Cultivating Adolescent Literacy

Cultivating Adolescent Literacy

Standards, Strategies, and Performance Tasks for Improving Reading and Writing

Gregory Berry

ROWMAN & LITTLEFIELD
Lanham • Boulder • New York • London

Published by Rowman & Littlefield
A wholly owned subsidiary of The Rowman & Littlefield Publishing Group, Inc.
4501 Forbes Boulevard, Suite 200, Lanham, Maryland 20706
www.rowman.com

Unit A, Whitacre Mews, 26-34 Stannary Street, London SE11 4AB

Copyright © 2017 by Gregory Berry

Every effort has been made to contact copyright holders for permission to reproduce borrowed material. We regret any oversights that may have occurred and would be happy to rectify them in subsequent printings of the work.

All rights reserved. No part of this book may be reproduced in any form or by any electronic or mechanical means, including information storage and retrieval systems, without written permission from the publisher, except by a reviewer who may quote passages in a review.

British Library Cataloguing in Publication Information Available

ISBN 978-1-4758-3810-7 (cloth : alk. paper)
ISBN 978-1-4758-3811-4 (pbk. : alk. paper)
ISBN 978-1-4758-3812-1 (electronic)

∞™ The paper used in this publication meets the minimum requirements of American National Standard for Information Sciences—Permanence of Paper for Printed Library Materials, ANSI/NISO Z39.48-1992.

Printed in the United States of America

Contents

Preface	ix
Acknowledgments	xi
Introduction	xiii

1 English Language Arts, Educational Reform, and the Common Core State Standards Movement — 1
- Cycles of Change — 1
- The Common Core State Standards: Promise and Controversy — 4
- Holding On to Literature in the English Curriculum — 10

2 Cultivating Literacy Skills through Close Reading — 17
- The Importance of Integrating Reading and Writing — 17
- Close-Reading Strategies for Literary and Informational Text — 19
  - Close Reading: What It Is and Why It's Important — 19
  - Close Reading Controversy — 21
- What Is Complex Text? — 23
- Suggested Close-Reading Strategies — 25
  - Strategy One: Four Basic Questions — 25
  - Strategy Two: Think Aloud — 25
  - Strategy Three: Vocabulary: Structural Analysis and Context Clues — 28
  - Strategy Four: Reading Like a Writer — 31
  - Strategy Five: Text Marking — 37

Strategy Six: Charting the Text	39
Strategy Seven: Interactive Shared Reading	42
Strategy Eight: Monitoring Comprehension	44
Strategy Nine: Multiple Readings	45
Strategy Ten: Using Evidence from Text	48
Strategy Eleven: Student-Determined Text-Dependent Questions	50
Strategy Twelve: Teaching Text Structure	52
Strategy Thirteen: Color Coding of Text	54
Strategy Fourteen: Commentary	56
Strategy Fifteen: Analyzing a Source	59
Strategy Sixteen: Paraphrasing	61
Strategy Seventeen: KNOWS	63
Strategy Eighteen: Apps to Promote Reading Skills	64
Strategy Nineteen: The One-Pager	66

3 Textual Evidence and Elaboration — 73
- Textual Evidence: What It Is and Why It's Important — 73
- Simple Ways to Teach Textual Evidence — 76
- Sample Strategies — 78
  - Color-Coding Strategy — 78
  - Poetry Explication: Supporting Your Reading by Citing Textual Evidence — 79
  - Using Transitions — 81
  - A Time to Dig Deeper: Answering Text-Based Questions — 87

4 Performance Tasks Designed for Specific Literary Texts — 91
- What Are Performance Tasks? — 91
- Performance Tasks for Specific Texts — 93
  - *Huckleberry Finn* and Nineteenth-Century Literature Performance Task — 93
  - *Cyrano de Bergerac* Performance Task — 98
  - *The Great Gatsby* Performance Task — 105
  - *Our Town* Performance Task — 109
  - *Of Mice and Men* Performance Task — 113
  - *The Crucible* Performance Task — 119
  - *Ricochet River* Performance Task — 122

The Bean Trees Performance Task	125
The House on Mango Street Performance Task	129
Poetry Performance Tasks	133
Part One: Literary Analysis of Theme	133
Part Two: Layered Curriculum	136
The Poverty Performance Task	139
Afterword: Letting Our Garden Grow	145
References	147
Index	151
About the Author	157

Preface

Spring is my favorite time of the year, when the air gets a little warmer and the days get gradually longer. New life begins to spring up everywhere as the buds on the trees begin to open and plants and flowers push themselves up through the cold ground. For many of us, it's time to think about the garden and spring planting. I find the gardening metaphor to be a compelling one for teaching literacy. Just as the ground needs to be tilled, fertilized, and readied for planting, the classroom environment needs to be cultivated and prepared for students to thrive and grow. A healthy literacy environment must be print rich, with a broad range of reading materials and teaching tools and an appropriate variety of teaching strategies and methods.

Just as the plants need to be fertilized, students need to be guided in finding that spark of inspiration and motivation. Tender seedlings, which must be nourished by sunlight, water, and fertilizer, are much like our students, who need to be exposed to good literature and quality reading material and taught how to use effective strategies for close reading and clear, coherent writing. Taking care of a garden is hard work. So is cultivating academic literacy skills in our students.

The success of our garden rests upon many integrated elements—the soil, the weather, the level of warmth, and the right amount of water, whereas the success of our students depends upon teachers carefully integrating reading and writing with other language arts skills and providing them with engaging strategies and performance tasks to nourish their growth as readers and writers. Occasionally, disease and blight may threaten the health of our garden, sometimes in the form of standardized assessments, district and state mandates, and unfair accountability measures. Yet we continue to try to do what we know is best for our garden. Just as the gardener tends the garden, trying to fix whatever stands in the way of the health of the flowers and vegetables, the effective teacher assesses, remediates, re-teaches, and builds her students' skills and leads them toward becoming not only literate but also lifelong learners.

Our schools must do whatever we can to cultivate deep literacy learning in our students, not just in English classes but also in every discipline and content area, across the curriculum, and with no exceptions. Literacy skills are too important to neglect in any area, and our students' future success, academically and in the workplace, depends on them. My argument has always been that literacy is not a part of learning or a single element of learning—literacy IS learning.

Imagine a classroom where the energy level is high; students are engaged in hands-on tasks with a variety of types of printed material and media; and small groups of students are working collaboratively, enthusiastically engaged in rigorous tasks that involve both close reading and analysis of challenging texts, including great pieces of literature, combined with purposeful and authentic writing. In this classroom, student literacy learning is being cultivated. We can and must teach students the skills they need to both independently and collaboratively deal with challenging reading and writing materials that they will face in college and in the workplaces of the future.

Acknowledgments

My deepest appreciation and thanks are extended to all those individuals who have played a role in the preparation, research, revision, and completion of this book. Thank you, as always, to my supportive and loving family members and friends. Thanks also to my colleagues in the Salem-Keizer School District for their friendship and support. Many of my colleagues have collaborated with me in the creation of the performance tasks and other materials included in this book, and I am very grateful for their contributions.

I would like to sincerely thank Dr. Tom Koerner, vice president and publisher at Rowman & Littlefield, for guidance and advice while serving as my editor, for seeing promise in this book, and for pushing me to make substantial and quality improvements in the manuscript. Also, thanks to Carlie Wall, associate editor at Rowman & Littlefield, for her help and patience and for being willing to answer an endless barrage of questions. I would also like to thank my former editor, Susanne Canavan, for helping me to formulate a vision and plan for this book and for reading early drafts of the manuscript and offering suggestions and encouragement. Thanks to Rowman & Littlefield for offering me the opportunity to complete this work and bring it to publication. Thanks also to the initial reviewers of the manuscript, who offered invaluable critique and suggestions for revision.

Special acknowledgments go to my colleagues and fellow teachers at South Salem High School and in the Salem-Keizer School District, especially my colleagues Cara Fortey, Matthew Isom, Sandy Graham, Joyanna Forsythe, Rebekah Sandusky, and Lauren Rasca. Many of these amazing teachers have collaborated in designing performance tasks and contributed other materials for this book. Some have also read and responded to early drafts of sections of the manuscript and provided helpful suggestions and critique. My colleagues have contributed much by simply engaging me in interesting conversations around reading, writing, and effective teaching.

I would like to extend additional thanks to my principal, Mrs. Lara Tiffin; Dr. Barbara Bamford, AVID coordinator and literacy specialist for Salem-Keizer Schools; Dr. Susan Lenski, professor of education at Portland State University; Assistant Principal Dr. Jeanette Morales; Karri Gordon, English teacher at North Salem High School; and the AVID Program for their contributions to this book.

I would like to acknowledge and honor all the hard-working English language arts teachers everywhere for their tireless efforts to cultivate literacy. And finally, my sincere gratitude for all of the great teachers I have had over the years, from my earliest years in elementary school to my professors in graduate school, who have taught me to appreciate and love teaching and learning and also inspired me to dedicate my life to cultivating literacy learning in my students.

Introduction

The purpose of this book is to offer middle and high school teachers some suggestions and strategies for cultivating rigorous literacy learning in their classrooms. Language arts teaching involves the teaching of many separate but interrelated skills: reading, writing, vocabulary, speaking, listening, and interpreting multimedia and multimodal texts. This book focuses primarily on approaches to reading and writing. It includes a variety of sample performance tasks and strategies that help nurture reading and writing in English language arts classes. It also discusses the role of ever-changing standards and our obligation to find ways of meeting them, and it emphasizes the power and importance of good literature in the ELA curriculum in the age of Common Core State Standards.

This book was written in a period where schools and teachers, at least in many states and regions of the country, are intently focused on meeting Common Core State Standards. Despite the controversy over them, Common Core State Standards do have much to offer. Yet the reality is, they are just another set of standards. Chapter One includes more discussion of the standards movement and Common Core, and Common Core Standards are referred to throughout this book, but the focus is primarily on ways to cultivate literacy, regardless of what set of standards have been prescribed. The primary purpose is to help you become an even more effective teacher by showing you some good strategies as well as some ways in which reading and writing can be integrated through a variety of types of performance tasks that provide students with rich, impactful learning of both skills and content.

Chapter One includes sections on CCSS and controversy surrounding them and also includes a section on the importance of the study of literature as the centerpiece of the language arts curriculum, with some rationale for holding on to literature in our curricula despite increased focus on reading of informational text. Chapter Two also focuses on strategies to promote close reading of text, both literary and informational. Chapter Three focuses on textual evidence and elaboration, with suggested strategies for teaching these skills.

The specific performance tasks included in Chapter Four are examples that teachers can use as models for their own curriculum; they include literary anchor texts and supplemental informational text combined with expository and argumentative writing. Included are several performance tasks associated with literary analysis and particular works of literature commonly taught (especially for American literature) as well as some suggestions for how teachers can create their own. My hope is that you will find this book to be a useful resource with lots of suggestions and strategies to cultivate literacy skills, one that you can pick up and begin using in your classroom tomorrow.

Chapter One

English Language Arts, Educational Reform, and the Common Core State Standards Movement

CYCLES OF CHANGE

Those of us who have been in the teaching profession long enough know very well that educational reform movements come and go. It's all too true that the pendulum swings and what was old becomes new again. Many of us, during our careers, have lived through initiatives such as open classrooms, flexible scheduling, integrated curricula, magnet schools, Goals 2000, Site-Based Decision Making, Quality Teaching, No Child Left Behind, the Smaller Schools movement, and the Professional Learning Community Model, and now Race to the Top, the Every Student Succeeds Act (ESSA), and the Common Core State Standards. You may also have seen various statewide initiatives come and go. Those of us here in Oregon also remember the Certificate of Initial Mastery (CIM) and Certificate of Advanced Mastery (CAM) in the 1990s.

Most of these movements have outlived their usefulness and been replaced with something new, but the reality is that in the world of education, we are always looking for the magic bullet, for better ways of doing things, and always trying to find a way to confront the challenges that have always faced schools in this great nation, the first to endeavor to meet the lofty goal of educating everyone: "The expansion of schooling to embrace all groups of children, regardless of background, throughout the 19th and 20th centuries is a trend-line of almost revolutionary proportions that has marked the United States as unique in the family of nations" (Cuban, 1990, p. 6).

Berliner and Glass (2015) argue that it is not possible for one program or reform to be universally successful; school improvement programs that work for some students and schools don't work for others, or may work in one area and not another. The reality is that if there was a magic bullet, we would have found it and implemented the perfect program for every state, district, and classroom (Berliner & Glass, 2015). In 1887, the great educational philosopher John Dewey (1972) wrote, "Moreover, the conditions of life are in continual change. We are in the midst of a tremendous industrial and commercial development. New inventions, new machines, new methods of transportation and intercourse are making over the whole scene of action year by year. It is an absolute impossibility to educate the child for any fixed station in life" (p. 59).

It seems that Dewey might as well be describing our own time in the second decade of the twenty-first century as much as his own late-nineteenth-century time. With the rapid increase of knowledge in the information age, amidst rapid globalization and along with ever-advancing forms of technology, we are again, in the first decades of the 21st century, left with the question of how best to educate our children. How do we know what skills students will need for the future when they will someday be working in career fields that do not even exist today?

One thing we can be sure of: our students will always need strong literacy and communication skills. The skills of reading, writing, speaking, and listening are essential learning and workplace skills, which will endure regardless of the time, place, or conditions. Our students will need to be good users of technology, good collaborators, good communicators, and good critical thinkers, and they must be comfortable with change, but first and foremost, they will need strong literacy skills. Whatever we can do to cultivate students' literacy skills today will benefit them in the long run, no matter what their futures hold.

In an article by Larry Cuban, published in *Educational Researcher* and titled "Reforming Again, Again, and Again," Dr. Cuban (1990) reflects on the reasons for the constant cycles of change and reform that are continual in the field of education. He makes several important points about school reforms, noting that a tendency toward constant reform has continued unabated since the early 20th century, and he also wisely observes that "reform visions often depend on a view of the past as a series of failures that killed a golden age of schooling" (p. 3). Cuban (1990) notes that deep and long-lasting debates about the forms of teaching in schools and varying educational values have created tensions about what schools should teach students and how.

Reforms seem to return again and again, and previous reforms failed to solve the problems they were supposed to have solved. The latest reforms are thus soon replaced with new reforms that seem eerily similar to reforms from past eras. Cuban (1990) notes that, especially since the end of World War II, school systems have faced unrelenting criticism about facilities, curricula, academic standards, and methods of teaching. The criticism is often highlighted by media attention, and schools are viewed as a "tool of reform when social problems emerge" (p. 8). Also, periods of economic instability and waves of social change cause the rise of various interest groups, whose interests are then turned into policy recommendation for schools (Cuban, 1990).

Remarkably enough, despite all the waves of change and school reform, over the years, schools and classrooms themselves have changed very little. Schools are left in a position of having to continuously mandate and promote new and novel reforms in an attempt to retain the support of critical constituencies (government, policymakers, governing bodies, communities, and so forth).

In his article, Cuban (1990) goes on to note that "inspections" in the form of teacher evaluation systems and standardized testing are the tools used to attempt to control what teachers do in their own classrooms. However, in the day-to-day work of teachers, there is, in reality, little oversight, and much is left to the professional judgment and craft of teachers as they attempt to determine what is best for their students. Cuban (1990) says: "The bureaucratic mechanism of inspection exists on paper, but it functions more as a ritual than as a tool for coordination and control" (p. 11).

Even today, when teachers face increasingly complex evaluation systems, value-added models, and the tying of student performance to teacher evaluations and, in extreme cases, to their paychecks, it remains true that the bureaucratic system is largely ritualistic, artificial, and not in line with the context of what really happens with students and teachers in classroom learning environments. So we do indeed keep reforming, again, again, and again, and solutions are often mismatched to the real problems that exist in education.

Cuban's article was written long before the Common Core State Standards and the movement toward national standards that they encompass, but make no mistake: Common Core is simply the latest in a continuing cycle of educational reforms that mandate more standardized testing and more complex evaluation mechanisms as the latest accountability measures in the continuing effort to improve and reform schools. Gorlewski and Gorlewski (2014), in *English Journal*, offer an even harsher critique of the current era:

> The Common Core, then, was originally designed as a tool of the political elite and the private sector. The Common Core was neither sought nor developed by educators or those who care about students or the future of the common good. The Common Core is meant for political gain and economic profit and is built on discourses of competition, business, and market value. This matters because the origin of a movement affects its implementation. Despite elevated rhetoric surrounding the Common Core, its underlying assumptions about what counts as knowledge, literacy, and culture will likely exacerbate—not ameliorate—inequality. (p. 12)

Good teachers recognize that we must be open to change, that we must embrace lifelong learning, and that our professional growth depends on our willingness to try new ideas and approaches, but many of us have recently become alarmed by the increasing trend toward standardization of both teaching and learning, toward greater homogenization, at the expense of individuality and creativity, which Common Core seems to promote.

Arpajian-Jolley (2014) acknowledges that growth requires change and as teachers we much change constantly, especially in terms of new approaches to teaching and new uses of technology in our classrooms. But she also notes that "it is time to rethink the current requirements for conformity. Educational decision makers these days suffer from myopia. They have lost a view of the whole picture of what an education should be: that it is more than math and language arts standards; that it is about developing productive adults who can make positive contributions to our democracy" (p. 84). The next section focuses on some of the controversy over and challenges presented by the Common Core movement.

THE COMMON CORE STATE STANDARDS: PROMISE AND CONTROVERSY

First, a little background on the Common Core State Standards. The Common Core is a set of academic standards in mathematics and English language arts/literacy (ELA) designed by the National Governors Association Center for Best Practices (NGA) and the Council of Chief State School Officers (CCSSO) (Council of Chief State School Officers, 2010).

These learning goals attempt to outline what a student should know and be able to do at the end of each grade. The standards were created with the lofty goal of ensuring that all students graduate from high school with the skills and knowledge necessary to succeed in college, careers, and life, regardless of where they live. Forty-three states and the District of Columbia originally adopted and most moved forward with implementing the Common Core State Standards. Some states and school districts, however, have come to question whether the standards are developmentally appropriate for all students nationwide, and they have withdrawn their support for the initiative. The CCSS Initiative has received criticism from both the political right and left. Several states that initially adopted Common Core have since voted to repeal or replace it.

Much of the concern swirling around Common Core has been due to the CCSS assessment systems, designed by two consortiums, the Partnership for Assessment of Readiness for College and Careers (PARCC) and Smarter

Balanced Assessment Consortium (SBAC). Valerie Strauss notes that many experts do not believe the assessments accurately measure the higher-order thinking required by Common Core Standards. She also notes that "member states are pulling out of the consortia and declaring that they are designing their own state tests, which threatens the notion of uniform assessments" (cited in Rycik, 2014, p. 53).

Many other educators have also questioned the appropriateness of the assessments, which require hours of testing time. Schools are scrambling to figure out how to find adequate computer lab space and time during the school schedule to fit in all the required testing time. In addition, "opt-out" movements (parents opting their children out of the standardized testing for Common Core assessment) have developed among parent and community groups around the country. Del Guidice and Luna (2013) observe that "parents and educators are rising in opposition to the plethora of new exams that will be used to assess student learning under Common Core Standards" (p. 22), and an organized campaign called United Opt Out National offers online guidelines for each state to help parents take advantage of their right to opt their kids out of taking the state tests.

In the field of education, standards are nothing new; we have always had some sort of standards that are used to guide instruction, so in that sense CCSS are not that unusual. Educational standards help teachers ensure their students have the skills and knowledge they need to be successful, while also helping parents understand what is expected of their children. However, many teachers believe that the Common Core Standards are excessively challenging and, at some grade levels, push students beyond their cognitive ability.

Teachers, as a general rule, do not object to standards because they provide us with direction and purpose for teaching. However, because standards drive assessment systems, it is the assessments that too often end up driving our curriculum, and we end up teaching to the test rather than spending our valuable class time cultivating solid learning, literacy, and critical thinking skills in our students. As Kelly Gallagher notes, "Pressures generated by the latest rounds of new standards and new testing are tempting teachers to abandon what they know is best for their children, sending both teachers and students down similar destructive instructional paths" (2015, p. 3).

According to policymakers, high standards that are consistent across states provide teachers, parents, and students with a set of clear expectations to ensure that all students have the skills and knowledge necessary to succeed in college, careers, and citizenship upon graduation from high school, regardless of where they live. These standards are also supposedly aligned to the expectations of colleges, workforce training programs, and employers, although some have also questioned this contention (Tienken, 2012).

The standards supposedly promote equity by ensuring all students are well prepared to collaborate and compete with their peers in the United States and abroad. Many educators, however, argue that the standards devalue creativity and innovation and encourage imitation and regurgitation. Tienken writes:

> Standardized reform policies raise homogenization above individualization and promote compliance instead of passion and interest. A system of standardization and centralization limits the pursuit of dreams and aspirations to those defined by state bureaucrats as important. Mimicking the convergent practices of totalitarian and authoritarian governments such as China and Singapore that constrict human thought and freedoms is not the way to foster the growth of an innovation economy or strengthen a democracy. (2014, p. 58)

Obviously, the widespread criticism and a range of viewpoints indicate a great deal of concern about the Common Core Standards. Critics also argue that several claims made by proponents of the Common Core are false, for example, the idea that the Common Core Standards are internationally benchmarked and grounded in research. In 2010, when the standards were being rolled out, five hundred early childhood experts—pediatricians, researchers, and psychologists—found the early childhood Common Core Standards to be so developmentally inappropriate that they called for their suspension in grades K–3 (Strauss, 2014).

This issue is one of the concerns about Common Core that Kelly Gallagher raises in his new book, that many of the grade-level standards are not developmentally appropriate. He gives an example of Literacy Standard 3, which asks elementary students to distinguish shades of meaning among related words that describe states of mind or degrees of uncertainty: "This reading standard asks students to think abstractly at an age when abstract thinking has not been developed. It requires a nuance that most students that age do not yet possess" (2015, p. 58). Beers and Probst (2013) observe, "New standards, without addressing old problems, won't change anything" (p. 25).

Another area of concern is the impact of Common Core State Standards on special education students and English language learners. Special education students, except those with severe cognitive disabilities, are also expected to meet the increased levels of rigor of the new standards, and the assessments will apply to them as well (Herbert, 2011). Some states, such as Florida, no longer approve modified courses where special needs students are not expected to cover as much material in the curriculum (Herbert, 2011). This higher level of expectation for special needs students is going to require greater levels of intervention and require that these interventions, and perhaps cut scores for CCSS testing, be written into students' individual education plans (IEPs).

Educators are also worried that the CCSS will negatively impact students whose native language is not English, which is the fastest-growing group of students in the country, currently about 10 percent of the total student population (Wingert, 2014). The CCSS standards and the guidelines presented for implementing them provide very little acknowledgment or understanding of the special challenges facing English language learners (ELLs).

The standards do give some general guidelines, such as using modified assessments and providing additional time, but as Coleman and Goldenberg (2012) note, the recommendations are vague and overly general. For example, in math, ELL students must be able to learn and discuss operations and proofs to come up with solutions to math problems, but "without those oral and written language skills, it is virtually impossible for students to have access to CCSS content" (Coleman & Goldenberg, 2012, p. 48). These students will need more content area literacy focus in disciplines such as math and science. English language learners will need to be supported by daily instruction in English language vocabulary, syntax, and conventions. They will also need lots of opportunities for academic conversation and verbal interactions with English speakers.

Critics of Common Core likely found reasons to celebrate on December 10, 2015, when President Obama signed into law the latest reauthorization of the Elementary and Secondary Education Act. The new law, called the Every Student Succeeds Act (ESSA), replaces No Child Left Behind and allows states considerably greater freedom in identifying their own goals and assessment. States will be required to implement academic standards, but they do not necessarily have to be the Common Core State Standards (The Every Student Succeeds Act: Explained). States must still test students in reading and math in grades 3–8 and once in high school, and the 95 percent participation rate still applies as well (The Every Student Succeeds Act: Explained). As of this writing, a new administration has taken over in Washington, which may bring about another round of new national reforms.

It is possible and likely that nationwide, the states that have already implemented the CCSS will keep them in place, regardless of the passage of the new education act, since many states and school districts have spent a great deal of time and money preparing for and implementing the Common Core: training teachers and staff, aligning curriculum, and purchasing textbooks and materials aligned to Common Core. It is unlikely most states and districts are going to simply abandon the Common Core.

Despite all the controversy over the CCSS, the new standards do raise the level of rigor and do have the potential to bring about positive changes in ELA education. Many educators have applauded the increased focus on literacy skills in all academic disciplines that Common Core mandates. The Common Core Standards have some potential to positively impact students' literacy skills in a variety of ways. Here are some of the shifts required by the Common Core State Standards.

Reading

The Common Core Standards require us to make several shifts in thinking about reading, one of which is a greater focus on careful examination of pieces of text. Students are expected to be able to read complex text closely and analytically and draw evidence from it. The same principle applies to all reading, regardless of the discipline: students must be able to draw evidence and knowledge from textual material. Strategies such as the ones presented in this book will help cultivate students' skills in close reading of complex texts, helping them to comprehend and gain insight from challenging reading material.

Also, as students advance through each grade, there is an increased level of complexity in what students are expected to read, and there is also a progressive development of reading comprehension. More close reading of increasingly complex texts through the grades is expected. There is no reading list to accompany the reading standards, which is a positive aspect in that teachers are left to make their own decisions about what literature and texts are appropriate for their students. However, students are expected to read a range of classic and contemporary literature as well as challenging informational texts from a variety of subject areas.

While gradually increasing the level of text complexity and increasing students' reading across the curriculum are laudable goals, many agree with Kelly Gallagher, who raises several concerns about the Common Core Reading Standards:

- There is little connection of the reading students do to the outside world (students must stay "within the four corners of the text").
- They undervalue, if not completely overlook, the importance of pre-reading activities.
- They ignore recreational reading.
- There are no reading targets (in terms of how much students should read).
- They may not be developmentally appropriate.
- They place too much emphasis on reading of informational text to the detriment of literary text.
- They overemphasize teaching of excerpts.
- The text exemplars provided are problematic. (2015)

Writing

While they include narrative and expository writing, the driving force of the writing standards is logical arguments based on claims, solid reasoning, and relevant evidence. The writing standards may help to sharpen students' writing skills in general, and they also insist on writing across the curriculum. The writing standards include opinion writing, even within the K–5 standards. Short, focused research projects as well as long-term, in-depth research is another component of the writing standards. Students are expected to write arguments, explanatory texts, and narratives across the grades. The standards also encourage teachers and students to use the writing process, and they acknowledge the interrelationship between reading and writing.

Speaking and Listening

Although reading and writing are the expected components of any English language arts curriculum, the core standards are written so that students gain, evaluate, and present complex information, ideas, and evidence specifically through listening and speaking. There is also an emphasis on academic discussion in one-on-one, small-group, and whole-class settings, which can take place as formal presentations as well as informal discussions during student collaboration. While it is good to see that the critical skills of listening and speaking, often neglected in language arts teaching, are included in the Common Core, the reality is that the testing systems that measure Common Core will evaluate students primarily in reading and writing. And since, as already noted, assessment drives teaching, it is unlikely that ELA curricula across the country will focus much greater attention on the skills of speaking and listening.

Language

The Common Core Language Standards also address vocabulary instruction, which the standards specify should take place through a mix of conversation, direct instruction, and reading so that students can determine word meanings and expand their use of words and phrases. They also focus on both academic vocabulary and domain-specific vocabulary (Standard L.6).

Media and Technology

Since media and technology are intertwined with every student's life, in and out of school in the twenty-first century, skills related to media use, which includes the analysis and production of various forms of media, are also included in these standards. The increased focus on these key twenty-first-century literacy skills will certainly have a positive impact on students' skills in comprehending and using multi-literacies.

Some teachers have found that aligning their curriculum to Common Core, rather than being a threat to teacher autonomy and student creativity, has actually increased the quality of their teaching and raised the level of rigor for their students. Lucy Boyd (2015) describes creating literature units with supplemental nonfiction texts for works such as Julia Alvarez's *In the Time of the Butterflies* and Shakespeare's *Romeo and Juliet*. She notes: "We chose key vocabulary words from each work and included discussion of broader concepts such as imperialism and internal oppression. We created lengthy writing assignments that asked students to compare and contrast nonfiction and fiction texts about the same topic" (p. 84). She notes that throughout the process of redesigning her curriculum, the CCSS provided a helpful resource in creating curriculum that would engage and challenge students. While Boyd (2015) does state that the CCSS are not perfect, she believes they can be a useful guide for redesigning curriculum and planning for effective teaching.

Unfortunately, there is no way to know for sure whether the Common Core State Standards move education in a positive direction, whether they will succeed in bringing about increased academic achievement, or, probably more likely, go the way of other school reform initiatives. The CCSS offer us lots of challenges and potential improvement in learning for students, but they may also result in increased student discouragement and failure. And worst of all, accountability measures tied to Common Core may be used by politicians and special interest groups to attempt to further discredit public education. We need some accountability for teachers and schools, but we also need to demand responsibility from parents, politicians, and the public.

Gallagher (2015), whose new book is appropriately titled *In the Best Interest of Students*, expresses his concern that "teachers are becoming so hung up on teaching every new standard that they are losing sight of the core literacy needs of our students" (p. 7). The best thing teachers can do is what we know works best: meet students where they are, assess their skills, and provide them with rich, positive learning experiences to cultivate their literacy skills and move them into higher levels of thinking and learning. The next section discusses the important role of literature in cultivating our students' literacy learning.

HOLDING ON TO LITERATURE IN THE ENGLISH CURRICULUM

Many English language arts teachers have expressed serious concerns about changes that have recently been imposed on their course curricula, supposedly mandated by CCSS. Because Common Core calls for a significant increase in the amount of informational text that students are required to read so that 70 percent of students' reading by the time they reach high school is made up of informational text, many administrators and teachers have assumed that this means less literature should be taught in English language arts courses. Many ELA teachers have revised their curriculum to add additional pieces of informational text and literary nonfiction to supplement literary reading. State departments of education and school superintendents have told schools to reduce the number of full-length literary works students read and replace them with shorter excerpts and more informational text (Stotsky, 2013).

In some schools English teachers have been told that all ELA courses must follow the 70/30 ratio of informational to literary text. Some high school ELA teachers have been told that 50 percent of student reading in their English classes must be informational text. Some middle school ELA teachers have been told they may no longer teach full-length novels and that students must only focus on close reading of shorter pieces of text. Some teachers have been disciplined for daring to teach a complete novel in their courses. These examples illustrate an egregious misinterpretation of the Common Core State Standards, and English teachers should and must fight to hold on to literature in our curriculum.

Too many people have misinterpreted the intentions of the Common Core State Standards. The authors of CCSS clearly state that imaginative literature should be emphasized in high school English classes, and it should be obvious to everyone that, in English courses, students should read predominantly literary text. Sandra Stotsky asks, "Why do teachers and administrators continue to think that the 50/50 division of reading standards at every single grade level means that about 50% of what English teachers teach in the classroom must be informational or literary nonfiction?" (p. 39). This is a very good question. Are math and science teachers being told that they must teach 50 percent literary text in their classes? Obviously not. If literature is not being taught to students in their English courses, where is it being taught?

First, let's look at what the authors of Common Core say regarding literary and informational text. The Revised Publishers' Criteria for the Common Core State Standards in English Language Arts and Literacy, Grades 3–12 state that students should have the opportunity to practice close reading of novels, plays, and full-length readings: "Students should also be required to read texts of a range of lengths—for a variety of purposes—including several longer texts each year. . . . Focusing on extended texts will enable students to develop the stamina and persistence they need to read and extract knowledge and insight from larger volumes of material (Coleman & Pimentel, 2012, p. 4). They are not suggesting that English teachers no longer teach full-length novels and plays.

The Revised Publishers' Criteria also state that for grades 6–12 English language arts courses, the balance of reading materials should include substantially more literary nonfiction, "to include a blend of literature (fiction, poetry, and drama) and a substantial sampling of literary nonfiction, including essays, speeches, opinion pieces, biographies, journalism, and historical, scientific, or other documents written for a broad audience" (Coleman & Pimentel, 2012, p. 5). However, in grades 9–12, they note that students should read not only historical documents but also American literature, world literature, a play by Shakespeare, and an American drama (Coleman & Pimentel, 2012). They also state that materials should be aligned throughout grades 3–12 to provide a "sequence of texts (of sufficient complexity and quality) to give students a well-developed sense of bodies of literature (like American literature or classic myths and stories) as part of becoming college and career ready" (Coleman & Pimentel, 2012, p. 6).

Many of us have long advocated for including a variety of types of texts, including nonfiction and informational text in our ELA classes, mainly because much of the reading students will do in college and in the real world will be informational text; however, literature has always been the cornerstone of English language arts, and it should remain so. The experience of reading literature cannot be replaced by any number of pieces of informational text. At the high school level, English is a content area, and literature makes up much of that content.

Part of the misconception among some district leaders and teachers is regarding the 70/30 split between informational and literary text recommended by CCSS. The 70/30 guideline is for *all* of the reading that students do during their school day, not just the reading done in English courses. So let's do the math. If high school students are taking somewhere between four and six academic subjects, and assuming they are doing lots of reading in all their classes, then only about 20 percent of their reading is in English class. We can also assume that most all of the reading done in their other classes would be informational text. So where do we come up with 30 percent of their reading being literary text? Wouldn't that mean that *all* the reading they do in English courses would have to be literary text? And they would still be about 10 percent short of the recommended 30 percent of literary text. As most of us know, while literary text can be used in several disciplines outside of English, especially history and the social sciences, the reality is that most non-English courses in middle and high schools do not include reading of literary text.

In his book *In the Best Interest of Students*, Kelly Gallagher (2015) raises several concerns about the shortcomings of Common Core State Standards, including this very misinterpretation regarding the amount of literary text in ELA courses. He argues: "Giving students fewer literary works to read is not in their best interest" and that literary reading "develops the mind in unique ways because the thinking that is generated through the reading of literary works is different from the thinking that is generated by reading in other disciplines" (p. 59). Beers and Probst (2013) also discuss some of the research in psychology and brain science, which reveals that the effects of reading literary fiction are greater than merely reading for pleasure and that reading literature actually helps us learn more about ourselves and others and how to relate to other human beings.

Literacy and English teachers must make a strong case and fight to hold on to literature in English language arts curriculum. Gallagher (2015) is correct when he states: "Literature and poetry have always been at the center of a strong ELA program, and they should remain so. No one would tell math teachers they should no longer teach algebra, and no one should be telling ELA teachers to cut back on the reading of literature and poetry. This trend of moving students away from literary reading is antithetical to good ELA instruction. Kids need more literary reading, not less" (p. 59). They also need exposure to a variety of challenging, classic literary texts and well-known authors and poets. Stotsky (2013) also notes that "the reduction of literary study will lead to fewer opportunities for students to acquire the general academic vocabulary needed for college work, especially if English teachers give them contemporary informational texts with a simplistic vocabulary to read in place of these older staples" (p. 7).

In the book *With Rigor for All: Meeting Common Core Standards for Reading Literature*, Carol Jago (2011) advocates for an ELA curriculum where students read both classic and contemporary literary texts. She notes, "Rich literature allows students to appreciate the universality of the human experience" (p. 67). Jago believes that we should teach the literary canon with direct instruction that provides support and scaffolding for modern students, who tend to spend most of their time on their various electronic devices, which has decreased the amount of time they spend reading literary text (Jago, 2011). We must provide instruction that will help students practice and learn techniques for how to read challenging texts, which will not only help them cultivate literacy skills but also enrich their lives in many ways.

While literature should always be the cornerstone of English coursework, there are also lots of opportunities to include literary nonfiction and informational texts to supplement the literature we are teaching. The performance tasks in Chapter Four of this book include several nonfiction reading selections to supplement the longer literary works that serve as anchor texts for the particular task. In many ways, this strengthens our curriculum and improves the rigor of the task, especially when students are asked to draw from a wide variety of texts as sources of evidence for completing a project, writing an essay, or making an argument.

Literature is a critically important part of students' education, and it is important to provide our students with a rationale for why they should spend time reading literature. When teaching a course that is literature based, you might begin with an introductory lecture/discussion to provide some basic information and an overview of the nature of literary study. In this introductory material, include some of the reasons why people read literature and why they, students, should also read and value literature. Ask students what makes a piece of writing good literature. After hearing them brainstorm some ideas, point out that the real indicator of good literature is that it is universal and transcends geographic boundaries. It has stood the test of time and is still found to be meaningful by later generations.

Many students today do not spend enough time reading, and there are many reasons why students should do as much reading as possible in school and in their daily lives in order to develop their literacy skills and become literate adults. In his book *Reading Reasons*, Kelly Gallagher (2003) presents and discusses nine excellent "reading reasons" that we can use to help motivate students to become better readers, among them that reading is rewarding, builds a mature vocabulary, makes us better writers, makes us smarter, is financially rewarding, and opens the door to college and beyond.

All of these are very good reasons why students should read as much as possible, but they apply to all types of reading—that is, reading in general. What about the student who asks, "Why do I have to read novels and poetry?" Teachers should be able to answer these questions for students and for ourselves: What are some of the reasons why literary study should be valued? Why should students read great stories, poetry, and plays? Why should we resist the forces that are trying to take literature out of our English classrooms and replace it with informational text?

As we observe what is going on in our own schools, districts, and states and noticing the push toward more informational text, we must reconsider why literature is important and why the bulk of students' reading in ELA classes should be literary text. Here are ten important reasons why we MUST hold on to literature in the ELA curriculum:

1. Literature has the power to affect us in ways that other forms of writing and communication do not. Kennedy and Gioia (2010) state that storytelling "affects us differently from other modes of language. We hear or read a story with the fullness of our humanity—not merely with intellects but also our emotions, intuition, and physical senses" (p. xvii). Some truths can only be told as stories, and narrative was our earliest way of making sense of the world around us.

2. Literature helps us better understand other people as well as ourselves; it expands our ability to understand other people and why they do the things they do, and thus to better understand ourselves. Reading literature expands our horizons and enriches us as human beings. Keith Oatley's research shows that reading literature actually improves our social skills by helping us understand others' viewpoints, builds empathy, and can even change our personalities. Narrative requires a different type of thinking than other written text (cited in Beers and Probst, 2013).
3. Literature helps us to appreciate diversity. Reading gives us the ability to vicariously experience and appreciate things that people of diverse cultures, eras, and parts of the world have done and experienced, thus building in us empathy and a sense of shared humanity. Students of all cultural and ethnic backgrounds need to see themselves reflected in the literature they read. A broad range of multicultural literature should be included in our curriculum. Literature also improves our understanding of ourselves, history, the social sciences, psychology, and other branches of knowledge. It allows us to "leap over the wall of self, to look through another's eyes" (Kennedy and Gioia, 2010, p. xviii).
4. Reading literature creates a greater sensitivity to language and the nuances of language. Writers of literary text, especially poetry, use language in more creative, dynamic, and unique ways than writers of other types of text, thus helping broaden students' understanding of the richness and power of language.
5. The reading we do improves our vocabulary, our writing, and our speaking skills. Reading literature increases students' vocabulary, both general and domain specific. Through the process of reading literature, we are constantly being exposed to and learning new words, thus improving our verbal and writing skills and helping us better understand fine shades of word meaning and the nuances of language use. Learning to write is largely a process of imitating the models we have seen and read. The pieces of literature students read provide models for student writing. Reading literature thus improves both our writing and speaking skills, in addition to making us better readers.
6. Reading literature expands our imagination and builds creativity; it helps us see and understand all the magical complexity of human beings and human behavior. It may even inspire us to try to use our creativity to write our own stories, poems, or dramas. It is the reading of literature that inspired many of the world's greatest authors. The next Charles Dickens, Walt Whitman, or Toni Morrison may be among your students today.

7. Literature helps us understand the universal human emotions and experiences, including love, hate, death, war, beauty, passion, heroism, loss, pain, pleasure, and so on. The great literary scholar Louise Rosenblatt (1976) wrote: "Whatever the form—poem, novel, drama, biography, essay—literature makes comprehensible the myriad ways in which human beings meet the infinite possibilities that life offers" (p. 8). Beers and Probst (2013) similarly observe, "It is imaginative literature that offers readers a chance to think about the human issues that concern us all: love, hate, hope, fear, and all the other emotions, problems, situations, and experiences of living" (p. 17).
8. Literature builds critical thinking skills. It teaches students how to analyze and critique the world around them, think about the ideas inherent in the literary works, and formulate their own viewpoints.
9. Literature helps us to think about issues in new ways and can empower students to take greater responsibility for the world around them. It builds social consciousness. In addition, because reading helps students understand the complexity of the world and humanity, they are more likely to move away from provincial, black-and-white thinking and formulate more realistic solutions to personal and real-world problems.
10. One of the most important reasons for having students read literature is perhaps one of the simplest: because it is pleasurable and provides an escape. People love to listen to stories, watch plays enacted on the stage, and hear poetry recited. It's fun to read Lewis Carroll's poem "Jabberwocky" and enjoy the poet's creative, playful use of language. For some students, the pleasure that literature can provide also provides a necessary escape from the harsh realities of their own lives and the world around them. Even if students don't choose to do much reading on their own or become the lifelong readers we would like them to be, we still want them to know something more about the world than just the town where they live and the lives of the small circle of people around them. Literature helps us understand where we come from and how we got to where we are.

Literature is invaluable and irreplaceable. No amount of reading of informational text can provide the same benefits that literary reading does. Literature is the centerpiece of the English language arts curriculum, the highest form of language study in any given language, and we must hold on to literature in our ELA curricula for the sake of our students.

Chapter Two

Cultivating Literacy Skills through Close Reading

THE IMPORTANCE OF INTEGRATING READING AND WRITING

There is an inherently close relationship between reading and writing. The skills and processes used when engaging in both activities are very similar. This interrelationship is evident in the fact that most students who are good readers are also good writers, and vice versa. In fact, all of the language arts skills—reading, writing, speaking, and listening—involve very similar processes in constructing meaning. We learn to read like writers and write like readers, and our reading helps to improve our writing and speaking.

Some research shows that when teachers use writing as a tool for learning, it leads students to higher reading achievement and also that using reading of text during the writing process also leads to better writing, helping students develop more effective cognitive strategies: "Reading and writing in combination have potential to contribute in powerful ways to thinking" (Tierney & Shanahan, 1991, p. 166). Therefore, an ideal way to help cultivate literacy learning is to provide students with lots of practice with integrated learning tasks, tasks that require them to engage in both reading and writing. This integrated approach is better than teaching reading and writing as separate and discrete skills.

Booth Olson (2003) recommends that, in teaching reading and writing together, we must build a bridge between the two through "instruction that actively uses one composing process to inform and illuminate the other. . . . As the students use writing to enrich their reading, and as they reread to dig deeper and enhance their writing, they learn to use their cognitive tool kit to craft meaning confidently and competently" (p. 393). This integrated approach is enhanced even further when we allow students to take ownership of their learning, use appropriate levels of texts and materials, provide adequate structure in the learning task, and encourage and facilitate collaboration among students. After some initial scaffolding, students will be able to internalize the process and become more autonomous learners (Booth Olson, 2003).

The Common Core State Standards offer many opportunities to integrate the various language arts skills. Although reading and writing standards are separated in the Common Core, a close relationship between them is implied. The CCSS have attempted not only to take a cross-disciplinary approach to literacy learning but also make use of an integrated literacy model. The standards for grades 6–12 are divided into four separate categories of Reading, Writing, Speaking and Listening, and Language; however, the interrelationship and close connection among all these communication skills is reflected. Research skills and multimedia are also integrated into the language standards, moving beyond the more traditional, primary skills of reading and writing.

For example, Anchor Standard 1 for Reading states that students must "Read closely to determine what the text says explicitly and to make logical inferences from it; cite specific textual evidence when writing or speaking to support conclusions drawn from the text." The authors of the standards make clear that they intend for students to use reading of textual materials to support writing and speaking. Almost any of the ten reading standards could be used to generate writing prompts to go along with the reading tasks. For example, in Reading Standard 9, students are asked to "Analyze how two or more texts address similar themes or topics in order to build knowledge or to compare the approaches the authors take." This standard lends itself to a comparison-contrast writing prompt using two different texts, perhaps on the same topic or with the same theme.

As another example, for Grades 9–12, Writing Standard 9 requires students to "Draw evidence from literary or informational texts to support analysis, reflection, and research." This standard clearly articulates that the grades 9–12 reading standards be applied to literature as well as literary nonfiction. To meet this standard, students have to engage in close, analytical reading of multiple texts and use them as evidence for their written work. For the Speaking and Listening Standard 4, at Grades 9–10, students must "Present information, findings, and supporting evidence clearly, concisely, and logically such that listeners can follow the line of reasoning and the organization, development, substance, and style are appropriate to purpose, audience, and task." Again, the standard makes clear that students are expected to share findings from their research in a clear and coherent way in a speaking task.

The Language Standards for Grades 6–12 also take an integrated approach. Language Standard 3 for Grades 6–8 requires that students "Use knowledge of language and its conventions when writing, speaking, reading, or listening," and for grades 10–12, "Apply knowledge of language to understand how language functions in different contexts, to make effective choices for meaning or style, and to comprehend more fully when reading or listening." Language Standard 6, which addresses vocabulary acquisition and use states that students must "use accurately general academic and domain-specific words and phrases, sufficient for reading, writing, speaking, and listening at the college and career readiness level" by grades 9–12. It is clear that the CCSS recognize the importance of integrating the various language arts skills.

Several of the strategies discussed and the performance tasks described in later sections use an integrated approach to literacy learning by combining reading of an anchor text and supplementary informational and nonfiction texts with specific writing tasks. The integrated approach will better serve to cultivate students' literacy learning.

The next section focuses on where we must begin: helping students develop strategies for close reading so they can read, comprehend, and respond to a variety of types of text.

CLOSE-READING STRATEGIES FOR LITERARY AND INFORMATIONAL TEXT

Close Reading: What It Is and Why It's Important

Listening to all the discussion surrounding Common Core State Standards, one would think that "close reading" is a revolutionary new breakthrough in teaching and learning. However, close reading is nothing new. Good English teachers and teachers in many other disciplines have been teaching their students how to do close reading for a long time. It has also long been an integral part of some approaches to literary criticism and a strategy used across disciplines. The Common Core State Standards, however, have brought renewed attention to close reading, with their emphasis on the importance of "close reading of complex text." Regardless of whether you are required to use Common Core State Standards in your teaching, close reading is still a critically important skill that we must teach. There are many great strategies presented in this section that teachers can use to help students practice close reading in order to better comprehend a variety of types of text.

So what is close reading? The ability to closely read and analyze textual material is a critically important skill for students, and the Common Core

State Standards place high priority on "close, sustained reading of complex text" at all grade levels (Coleman and Pimentel, 2012, p. 4). The authors of Common Core define close reading as "what lies within the four corners of the text," and they recommend using shorter pieces of text to allow students to "read and re-read deliberately and slowly to probe and ponder the meanings of individual words, the order in which sentences unfold, and the development of ideas over the course of the text" (Coleman and Pimentel, 2012, p. 4). They also note that, to build reading skill and become college and career ready, students must "grapple with a range of works that span many genres, cultures, and eras and model the kind of thinking and writing students should aspire to in their own work" (Coleman and Pimentel, 2012, p. 5).

Frey and Fisher (2013) note that close-reading strategies should be used with complex texts that require "repeated reading and detailed investigation" (p. 45). Close reading involves the kinds of skills that students use during active reading of a text to help them uncover layers of meaning in the text and thereby come to a full comprehension of the author's ideas and techniques. One of the Common Core assessment consortiums, the Partnership for Assessment of Readiness for College and Careers (PARCC), offers a very useful definition of close reading:

> Close analytic reading stresses engaging with a text of sufficient complexity directly and examining meaning thoroughly and methodically, encouraging students to read and reread deliberately. Directing student attention on the text itself empowers students to understand the central ideas and key supporting details. It also enables students to reflect on the meanings of individual words and sentences; the order in which sentences unfold; and the development of ideas over the course of the text, which ultimately leads students to arrive at an understanding of the text as a whole. (2011, p. 7)

Another important aspect, or perhaps an outcome, of close reading is the ability to compare and synthesize multiple sources. Making connections and comparisons among texts helps students to build a greater understanding of the subject of study.

We also need to consider the importance of inquiry and motivation as factors in close reading. When readers have questions, are looking for information, or are trying to solve a problem, they depend on close-reading strategies to accomplish their goals. Teachers need to provide a purpose for student reading and find ways to motivate them to engage in the hard work of close reading. Many students can read and comprehend just fine, but they may choose not to because they lack necessary motivation. The missing piece is often motivation and engagement. Motivation might involve tapping into student interests and prior learning and experience but also requires strategies that will help engage students in the content (Brophy, 2010). It might also involve removing barriers that prevent students from being successful, such as helping them understand challenging vocabulary prior to reading as well as helping them make connections between the content material and their own lives and experiences.

Every reading lesson and task must involve motivating students to engage in close reading. Cole (2014) presents six suggestions for motivating students to engage in close reading: choosing engaging texts, beginning with essential questions that will serve to set the stage and motivate students, reading aloud to and with students, providing choice through reading workshops and literature circles, ensuring learning with closure by helping students make personal connections and making homework meaningful, and finally, celebrating accomplishments. Cole (2014) notes, "Without a good reason to read, motivation to close read or reread will not happen" (p. 23), and also "an instructional stance focused on motivation and engagement will help teachers provide excellent instruction and enable students to read closely in order to learn" (p. 26).

It is also important to note that close reading should not be the exclusive realm of ELA courses. Close-reading strategies should be used widely across disciplines and anytime students are engaged in reading any complex text. Close reading is a disciplinary task that allows for knowledge within the various disciplines to be understood, processed, and produced. For example, historians engage in close reading of primary documents and sources, mathematicians use close reading of number and symbol systems, and scientists use close reading of sets of data, lab results, and scientific articles and reports. In the English language arts, the purpose of our close reading is often to analyze authorial craft.

Several of the strategies in this section promote close reading of literary text to analyze craft and structure. Coleman and Pimentel (2012) recommend using "text-dependent" questions that will help students understand specific aspects and techniques being used by the writer as well as collaborative discussions to help students learn to engage with and respond to the ideas expressed by their peers.

Close Reading Controversy

The CCSS authors' admonition that readers be taught to stay "within the four corners of the text" and read unfamiliar textual material without drawing upon prior knowledge has been somewhat controversial. If taken literally, staying within the four corners of the text would mean that there is no provision for making personal connections to the text or connecting the reading material to the outside world. Gallagher (2015) expresses his concern about this notion, arguing that "stopping inside the four corners of the text limits our students' thinking" (p. 50). Beers and Probst (2013) also note that the Common Core presents a "narrow vision of close reading."

Literary scholar Louise Rosenblatt (1976) was one of the earliest scholars to articulate an important concept in reading comprehension: that the reading process is one involving a transaction between reader and text in which the reader makes connections between prior knowledge and new information. Beers and Probst (2013) also suggest that close reading is that which should "bring the text and the reader close together" (p. 36). In an article called "Seven Traps of the Common Core State Standards," Karen Eppley (2015) argues that the way close reading is presented in the Publishers' Criteria is a distortion of what reading really is and that "the attempt to reduce reading to a process of determining what the print says is inadequate as a singular conceptualization of what it means to read and silences the potential that books have to engage adolescents with the social contexts within which they are set and read" (p. 209).

It is unreasonable to expect that readers will always stay within the four corners of the text. As teachers, we want students to be able to draw upon their background knowledge in interpreting text, which is a critical element of what good readers do. We also want them to move outside of the text to think about real-world implications, gain greater insight, and make connections to other texts, ideas, events, and topics. In addition, for struggling readers, encountering and grappling with a piece of difficult reading material on their own and without being able to draw upon pre-reading activities or prior knowledge is a bridge too far. To illustrate this concept, let's examine a short passage from a recent news article from the *Wall Street Journal*:

> Federal Reserve officials face a conflict as they plan to start raising interest rates later this year. There has been a lot of progress in their goal for U.S. job growth, but little in their objective of modestly raising consumer prices.
>
> The central bank on Wednesday left its benchmark short-term interest rate near zero—for the 2,417th straight day—but dropped several hints after a two-day policy meeting that is near seeing enough improvement in the job market to prompt officials to raise the rate as early as September. (Hilsenrath, 2015)

Now imagine a student, especially a struggling reader, trying to comprehend this excerpt but staying only within the four corners of the text. To comprehend this passage, the reader must draw upon some prior knowledge about the financial system and how it works. A lack of background knowledge is often a substantial hindrance for readers. It would be critical to preview this article for students, to identify what the Federal Reserve is, and explain some basic economic principles of the financial system. Students would also need to have some understanding of the interest rate and its impact on job growth and consumer prices.

We want all of our students to reach the point of being able to independently and confidently read and comprehend complex pieces of literature and informational text. That should be the ultimate goal of teaching in any discipline that requires students to read. One way to build this confidence and competence is to teach students active reading strategies and help them generate questions of their own. Several of the strategies presented in this section help us move students closer to the goal of being able to independently read and interpret complex text. As Beers and Probst (2013) state, "We want them to notice those moments that trigger their own memories and thoughts about their own lives, about other texts they have encountered, and about events in the world. And we hope to see them pausing there to reflect, to articulate the questions that arise, and to speculate about possible answers and explanations" (p. 5).

As readers, all of us bring our own experiences to what we read. Good readers ask questions, make connections to ourselves and others, and make predictions, and ultimately our reading becomes more meaningful and purposeful. Indeed, viewing the reading process as merely decoding the meaning of the text and what lies within the four corners of the text will cause us to reduce reading instruction to a guessing game of right and wrong answers where students are expected to figure out what the teacher thinks is the right answer and where one reader's interpretation is the only one allowed.

Beers and Probst (2013) describe this approach as a "question and answer session in which the teacher drags the class through her interpretive steps only, preventing them from seeing the text in any way other than the way in which she has construed it" (p. 37). Textual material is nothing but ink spots on a page until someone reads it and interprets it. Reading should involve, as Rosenblatt noted (1976), a transaction between the reader and text in which readers bring their own experiences and ideas to every new text they encounter.

WHAT IS COMPLEX TEXT?

It is important to understand what we mean by the term "complex text" as well as how text complexity is measured. Complex test usually refers to very dense material, which may have challenging language and vocabulary and a complex text structure that requires slow, deliberate reading and use of active reading strategies. The term "text complexity," as used by the authors of the

Common Core, means more than just readability levels that provide a general reading Lexile or grade-level band for particular texts. Common Core uses three factors to measure text complexity:

- Quantitative indicators: readability indicators that place a text within a certain grade-level band in terms of word length and frequency, average sentence length, and so forth.
- Qualitative indicators: aspects of text including meaning, structure, language conventions, and knowledge demands placed on the reader for him or her to understand the text.
- Matching readers with texts and tasks: reader and task variables, such as motivation, readers' background knowledge and experience, students' levels of cognitive ability, and the particular task assigned (Frey & Fisher, 2013).

Quantitative measures alone are not enough because there are too many other variables. Readability can be affected by text structure, genre, organization, use of graphics, and level of ambiguity within the text. Literary text in particular may be at a lower level of complexity when measured by qualitative measures but may actually be much more challenging in terms of subject matter, themes, and literary elements. Perhaps the most important indicator of the three is appropriately matching readers with texts. Readability can be affected by the particular reader's maturity and readiness for dealing with the subject matter and her or his general cognitive ability. Whenever selecting reading material for a particular class, a teacher should always consider these factors.

Another important element affecting readability is seldom discussed: student stamina. Students must be taught the strategies that good readers use to read challenging materials. This includes self-discipline and good study habits. If we are going to expect students to read a variety of textual material and synthesize information from multiple texts, we have to help them build the stamina required as well as help them to eliminate distractions and thereby focus their attention on the text for a necessary period of time. This ability to focus is also influenced, of course, by their level of motivation, general work ethic, maturity, and willingness to engage with challenging academic materials. We need to constantly come back to Gallagher's (2003) reading reasons and try to motivate students by showing them why reading is the most important skill they can master. Although it is hard, it is necessary.

One more point about close reading: it often involves repeated readings of the same text. Many students have never been taught how to do this or why it is important. Many students, when assigned reading material, read quickly, do not know how to use active reading strategies, do not think about what they are reading, end up bored and apathetic about the material, and fail to adequately comprehend. Slowing down and taking time to re-read the text does not cross their minds. It may never occur to them that even good readers have the same problems they do but have learned how to monitor their comprehension, slow down, and re-read where necessary.

As a result of their lack of active reading strategies, students often can't remember what they have read, many do not perform well academically, and many of them fail to pass the mandated high-stakes tests that are often required for graduation. Most all students can read—they can decode the text—but most simply have never learned how to engage in rigorous reading. We must provide them with some strategies to help them reach higher levels of success when reading complex text. The strategies that follow have been designed with the intent of cultivating students' close-reading skills to help them understand and fully appreciate complex text.

SUGGESTED CLOSE-READING STRATEGIES

Strategy One: Four Basic Questions

A simple close-reading strategy suggested by Boyles (2013) is to teach students to ask four basic questions after reading a short portion of any text:

- What is the author telling me here?
- Are there any hard or important words?
- What does the author want me to understand?
- How does the author play with language to add to meaning?

These four questions are potentially very useful because they help students to address several important aspects of close reading. The first question addresses literal comprehension; the second, vocabulary; the third, inferential comprehension; and the fourth, the author's craft and use of language (particularly useful with literary text). Boyles (2013) suggests that if students learn to ask these questions, they will become more skillful at answering them, and their ability to analyze complex text will increase. We can apply this strategy with the previously quoted excerpt from the *Wall Street Journal* article (see figure 2.1).

Strategy Two: Think Aloud

The think aloud has been a commonly used strategy for some time, but it is one of the most effective strategies that teachers can use to demonstrate to students how to use active reading strategies to comprehend complex text. The think-aloud strategy was originated by Davey (1983). It can help teach students to analyze the author's use of language, make predictions, ask questions, explore the title, and visualize. The think aloud is a simple technique where the teacher models her thinking as she processes information about a

Question 1: What is the author telling me here?	The author is telling me that Federal Reserve officials are considering raising interest rates later this year due to improvement in the job market.
Question 2: Are there any hard or important words?	Words I need to understand: Federal Reserve, interest rates, consumer prices, benchmark, central bank, short-term interest rate, job market
Question 3: What does the author want me to understand?	The author wants me to understand that job growth and consumer prices are affected by interest rates, which are set by the Federal Reserve. The author also wants me to understand that it is likely that the interest rate will be increasing sometime soon.
Question 4: How does the author play with language to add meaning?	The author is a journalist who is focused on presenting the most important information in the very first paragraph. He shows the conflict that Federal Reserve officials face. He also uses the term "benchmark" to describe the position of short term interest rates. He uses dashes in order to emphasize how long the interest rate has been left near zero (2,417 days).

Figure 2.1. Four Basic Questions

particular text, doing so out loud while students are reading along in the text. Berry (2014) presents a five-step process for the think aloud:

- Explain to students that good readers ask themselves questions while they are reading to help understand what they are reading.
- Use a passage from a piece of complex text, an excerpt from the textbook, an article, a poem, or some other piece of text. Prepare for the read aloud by marking your own copy of the text, noting particular passages and features that students are likely to find difficult. Also, note difficult vocabulary or terminology and likely points of confusion. Before the lesson, write out a few questions you can ask yourself to show your thinking as you read the text.
- Have students read the text silently while you read it aloud. During your reading, stop to verbalize your thinking, ask questions, and show the process that you are using to understand the text: "What does this section heading mean?" "Why does the author use this particular term?" "I predict that the next thing the author will discuss is. . . ." Also, note points where you are confused: "I didn't understand this part very well so I'm going to go back and re-read it."
- Try to model all of the following active reading strategies during your think aloud: making predictions, describing mental pictures you develop, noting connections to your prior knowledge, creating comparisons and analogies, and showing where your comprehension breaks down and you need to re-read.

- Once you have modeled the process a few times, have students work with a partner to practice doing think alouds of their own. Ask for students to volunteer to demonstrate a think aloud for the whole class. Finally, revisit this strategy several times so students can begin to imitate the practices of the think aloud in their own reading.

To illustrate the think aloud, let's look at the opening passage from George Orwell's classic novel *1984* (1949):

> It was a bright cold day in April, and the clocks were striking thirteen. Winston Smith, his chin nuzzled into his breast in an effort to escape the vile wind, slipped quickly through the glass doors of Victory Mansions, though not quickly enough to prevent a swirl of gritty dust from entering along with him.
>
> The hallway smelt of boiled cabbage and old rag mats. At one end of it a colored poster, too large for indoor display, had been tacked to the wall. It depicted simply an enormous face, more than a meter wide: the face of a man of about forty-five, with a heavy black mustache and ruggedly handsome features. Winston made for the stairs. It was no use trying the lift. Even at the best of times it was seldom working, and at present the electric current was cut off during daylight hours. It was part of the economy drive in preparation for Hate Week. The flat was seven flights up, and Winston, who was thirty-nine, and had a varicose ulcer above his right ankle, went slowly, resting several times on the way. On each landing opposite the lift shaft, the poster with the enormous face gazed from the wall. It was one of those pictures which are so contrived that the eyes follow you about when you move. BIG BROTHER IS WATCHING YOU, the caption beneath it ran. (pp. 1–2)

(Excerpt from *Nineteen Eighty-Four* by George Orwell. Copyright © 1949 by Houghton Mifflin Harcourt Publishing Company, renewed 1977 by Sonia Brownell Orwell. Used by permission of Houghton Mifflin Harcourt Publishing Company. All rights reserved. World rights: *Nineteen Eighty-Four* by George Orwell. Copyright © George Orwell, 1949. Reprinted by permission of Bill Hamilton as the Literary Executor of the Estate of the Late Sonia Brownell Orwell.)

While reading this opening passage with students, here are the questions you might ask and the statements you might make aloud while reading:

- The first paragraph provides the setting of the story, noting that it is April and set in a place called Victory Mansions. It also names Winston Smith, who is probably the main character since most authors identify the main character right away.
- What does "vile" mean? I think it means something unpleasant or bad.
- The fact that the clocks were striking thirteen is unusual. First of all, clocks have only twelve numbers, so the use of thirteen suggests that perhaps this society uses military time.

28   Chapter Two

- The name "Victory Mansions" suggests a fancy apartment or condominium building, but this is contrasted with the "swirl of gritty dust," which suggests maybe it is not such a nice place.
- What is the purpose of the poster with the enormous face of a man? The author notes a few lines later that the poster of the man's face appears on every floor.
- The smell of boiled cabbage and old rag mats and the fact that the elevator doesn't work and the electricity is turned off during the daytime suggest that I was right that this building is run-down, old, and not a very nice place.
- What is a "lift"? I think lift is the British term for "elevator."
- Some additional details about the character Winston are given: he is thirty-nine years old, lives on the seventh floor, and has a varicose ulcer. I'm not sure what that is. I've heard of "varicose veins," so maybe it's similar.
- I'm going to go back and re-read the second paragraph to see whether there are any details that I missed.
- The narrator mentions that people are preparing for the "economy drive." I wonder what that means. Maybe it's something like a food drive or a community service day.
- Based on some of the details in this passage, I predict that the story is set in a future time period and perhaps is science fiction.
- "Big Brother Is Watching You" is the caption on the poster. The term "Big Brother" is often used today to suggest invasion of privacy, use of surveillance cameras, or government methods used to monitor people's behaviors and conversations. I bet this book deals with some of those themes of government control. I wonder whether the term "Big Brother" actually comes from this book?
- Winston notes that the eyes of the man on the poster seem to follow you as you move. I've noticed this with lots of pictures and paintings where the subject seems to be looking at the viewer and the eyes seem to follow. Maybe the leaders of this society want the people to feel that they are always being watched.

After modeling the think-aloud process a couple of times, ask students to do a pairs-read activity with a piece of text, taking turns practicing the think aloud for each other. You may also have an ambitious student who is willing to try doing his or her own think-aloud demonstration for the class.

Strategy Three: Vocabulary: Structural Analysis and Context Clues

Understanding of vocabulary is a critical component of good reading comprehension. One cannot discuss the concept of close reading without considering how good readers react when they identify unknown words while reading. One key feature of strong readers is they are very good at identifying words and word meaning while reading. Students with a low level of vocabulary knowledge will be greatly slowed by having to stop and analyze many of the words they are encountering in the text, which is a double-edged sword because they also lose the focus on the content and flow of the text due to having to stop so often. As students build reading skill, they learn and recognize more and more words. Remind students that the best way to improve their vocabulary is to gain as much reading practice as possible.

The term "structural analysis" refers to the ability to recognize words and identify their meaning by analyzing the structural units in the word. These include prefixes, suffixes, and root words. To teach students to read closely, we must teach them how to recognize word parts, model for them how to do this, and give them lots of independent practice. When readers come across unknown words, they should look at the word parts and see whether there are any of them they can identify. Take the time during your teaching to focus on some of the key vocabulary words and demonstrate for students how to analyze the structure.

Frey and Fisher (2013) use an example of a reader encountering the word "paleozoology." This word includes several morphological parts, including prefix, root, and suffix. If a reader is able to remember that "paleo-" means "old or ancient," "zoo" refers to animals, and "-ology" refers to the study of something, they are then able to identify the meaning of the term: "The study of ancient animals by examining fossils." Frey and Fisher (2013) note, however, that it is not enough to merely hand students a list of prefixes, roots, and suffixes; instead "teachers need to model the use of morphology in understanding words" (p. 29).

One class period, when doing a whole-group read aloud of a piece of text, you come upon the following word: "monophonic." You might say aloud something like the following:

> What does the term "monophonic" mean? Let's see if we can figure it out. You probably know what the prefix "mono-" means—only one. What does the root word "phon" or "phone" mean? "Phonics" refers to some type of sound, like music or recorded sound, a speaker, or even spoken language, like the word "microphone" refers to a small device for magnifying one's spoken words. The ending of the word, "ic," refers to the practice of doing something or pertaining to something, so "monophonic" means sound reproduction through one single method or channel. I've even heard the opposite of this term, which I believe is "stereophonic," or broadcast on multiple channels. I think this word is sometimes used as a musical term.

The other important element of vocabulary understanding is use of context clues. Looking at the specific context of the word can be valuable in understanding the meaning since context clues are often embedded in the text around a particular word or term. Sometimes, especially in content-area textbooks, synonyms and antonyms of a term are provided in the sentences themselves. Sometimes the word may be defined indirectly as well. It is also important to model the use of context clues for students to help them learn to use context clues themselves.

Here is an example: "The *Constitution*, which outlines the fundamental principles of how our nation is governed, is considered one of the most seminal and groundbreaking documents in American history, the first of its kind and a document giving birth to a new form of representative democracy."

In this sentence, the adjective clause "which outlines the fundamental principles of how our nation is governed" provides an actual definition of the word "constitution." This is true whether one is referring to the U.S. Constitution or some other nation's constitution. The word "seminal" is also followed by some context clues that are useful in determining its meaning. By associating it with another, somewhat similar term, "groundbreaking," we are provided with a suggestion that "seminal" refers to something new. This is followed by further clarification at the end of the statement: "the first of its kind and giving birth to a new form of representative democracy." Using these clues surrounding the word, one can develop a satisfactory understanding of how both of these terms are used in the sentence.

Here is another example: "My friend's ambiguous statements about the meaning of last night's events left me puzzled and confused." In this sentence, the word "ambiguous," which we can tell is an adjective because it ends in "-ous," is used to describe the "statements" made by the friend. The statements refer to the context of what happened last night, and since the writer of the sentence is left puzzled and confused, we can infer that the ambiguous statements made by the friend were not helpful but rather were confusing and unclear.

Sometimes, context clues are also provided in the form of contrasting ideas and nonexemplars, as in this example: "Altruism, contrary to selfishness and greed, is a rare and admirable quality." The phrase starting with "contrary to" provides the definition of the opposite of the term "altruism." Thus, the reader can interpret that "altruism" means "unselfish concern for the welfare of others."

Have students practice with the following sentence. See if they can find any context clues, restated ideas, synonyms, or examples that provide clues to the meaning of the terms "calamitous" and "resilient": "Having survived an earthquake, a flood, and a devastating wildfire, even these calamitous events could not defeat Robert's resilient spirit."

Here are some teaching tips for teaching structural analysis and context clues:

- First, model for your students how a good reader practices analyzing word parts and looks for context clues to word meanings. Do this with brief passages of text and excerpts from reading assignments, during think alouds, and anytime you are doing whole-group reading. Demonstrate for students how to ask questions about the vocabulary, such as the following: What is the overall purpose of the sentence? What words and phrases in the sentence provide clues or suggestions as to the meaning of the word? What clues does punctuation provide (commas surrounding a phrase or the use of a dash, for example)? Does the writer provide any examples or illustrations that provide clues to the meaning of the term?
- If students are working on reading texts or articles in small groups, move around the room and ask students whether they have identified any challenging words in the text. Then demonstrate for them how they might try using structural analysis and context clues to identify the words. If neither approach is helpful, then it may be time to turn to a dictionary.
- Use tools such as graphic organizers, online resources, word games, and word walls to help students with vocabulary learning. The book *Literacy for Learning: A Handbook of Content-Area Strategies for Middle and High School Teachers* (Berry, 2014) includes a whole section of useful vocabulary strategies and lots of graphic organizers.
- Have students practice identifying context clues by asking them to highlight or write down examples of context clues that they identify during their reading. Use this process with reading of online text. Also, having students work in pairs, highlight terms used and speculate about the meaning using context clues or analysis of word parts; then check their definition using www.dictionary.com.

Strategy Four: Reading Like a Writer

In his book *In the Best Interest of Students*, Gallagher (2015) refers to the concept of "reading like a writer." This concept provides a method for moving students toward deeper levels of reading, beyond just thinking about what the text says and means (the content) and toward focusing on the techniques the writer is using. It helps build an understanding of the writer's craft and structure (a major part of the Common Core Reading Standards). Gallagher (2015) suggests using questions such as the following:

- What makes this an effective piece of writing?
- What techniques are used by the writer that elevates the writing?
- What "moves" does the writer make?
- What does he do here? What does he do there? (pp. 31–32)

Recognizing the "moves" the writer makes means analyzing the techniques the writer uses. This may include the author's use of language, imagery, and descriptive detail; the organizational structure of the text; and many other elements. Let's focus specifically on how writers use sentence structure and punctuation. Often, students have difficulty comprehending text because they get lost in an author's sentence structure, especially if it is a long and complex sentence. Students often are unable to recognize how the parts of the sentence fit together. They need to be able to recognize how writers use clauses and phrases (the parts of the sentence) to create the meaning. Phrases, for example, are often used to describe a noun or verb in a sentence.

Also, you may often notice that students, especially struggling readers, tend to *read through the punctuation rather than reading with the punctuation.* In other words, when asked to read a sentence or passage aloud, they read it without the punctuation, as if the punctuation marks were not there. They will even read right through end punctuation and into the next sentence. This failure to observe the writer's use of punctuation can interfere significantly with comprehension and create confusion. Use short passages of text and have students read through them slowly, multiple times, noting and using all of the punctuation, pausing briefly for commas and coming to a complete stop at the end of sentences. This simple practice not only builds fluency but also improves comprehension.

As Gallagher (2015) observes, it is also important to teach students that writers can manipulate the punctuation "to bring additional meaning to the piece, that a writer can punctuate for reasons beyond correctness" (p. 33). This is especially evident when analyzing literary text, particularly poetry. For example, you might have students analyze the poetry of Emily Dickinson or e.e. cummings, both poets who are known for their unconventional use of punctuation and capitalization. Here is an example of the first lines from e.e. cummings's poem "i thank You God for most this amazing":

> i thank You God for most this amazing
> day: for leaping greenly spirits of trees
> and a blue true dream of sky; and for everything
> which is natural which is infinite which is yes
>
> (i who have died am alive again today,
> and this is the sun's birthday; this is the birth
> day of life and of love and wings: and of the gay
> great happening illimitably earth) (Sullivan, 1978, p. 480)

("I thank You God for most this amazing." Copyright 1950, © 1978, 1991 by the Trustees for the E. E. Cummings Trust. Copyright © 1979 by George James

Firmage, from *Complete Poems: 1904–1962* by E. E. Cummings, edited by George J. Firmage. Used by permission of Liveright Publishing Corporation.)

In this interesting poem, there are several things a reader should notice regarding the poet's use of capitalization, punctuation, and syntax:

- The only words cummings chooses to capitalize are in the first line: "You God."
- He does not capitalize the first words of stanzas or lines, as poets usually do.
- Each stanza includes four lines (quatrains). In the first stanza, the initial clause is followed by a colon. Following the colon is further explanation of the statement made in the first part, details such as "leaping greenly spirits" and "blue true dream of sky." This is then followed by a semicolon. In the second stanza, the colon and semicolon are reversed, with the semicolon first.
- Neither stanza ends with a period; in fact there are no periods used in the poem at all.
- The usual English syntax is often reversed by cummings: instead of "this most amazing," it is "most this amazing." Other examples include "leaping greenly spirits," "blue true dream," and "gay great happening."
- The entire second stanza is enclosed by parentheses.
- At the end of the first stanza is a series of items: "everything which is natural which is infinite which is yes." Normally, items or phrases are a series separated by commas, but cummings chooses not to use any commas here.

When discussing this example, or any other example of a poem or piece of literary text, it would be important to discuss with students each of these "moves" the poet makes. Why does he choose to use punctuation, capitalization, and sentence structure in this stylistic way, and how does that reflect the meaning in the poem or influence the reader's interpretation of the piece? You can use this technique with other genres, as well, and for both literary text and informational text.

To analyze an author's use of punctuation, it is important that students understand the common uses of various punctuation marks. Chances are, many of your students do not know how some marks of punctuation are correctly used, especially less common ones, like colons and dashes. Depending on your students' ability levels, it may be necessary to design some mini-lessons to teach them these marks of punctuation: commas, end punctuation (period, question mark, exclamation point), semicolon, colon, dash, parentheses, hyphen, apostrophe, and quotation marks. There are other less common forms of punctuation, such as slashes (virgules), brackets, asterisks, ampersands, and numerous symbols, but the most common forms of punctuation are listed here. You can use these excerpts as mini-lessons and perhaps provide a few practice sentences along with them:

- Comma (,): the most frequently used mark of punctuation, commas mark a pause in the sentence. They separate elements of a sentence, including words, phrases, and clauses. They are often used in pairs, such as in the following example: "My friend Vincent, the top student in the class, will be this year's valedictorian." This sentence includes an appositive phrase, "the top student in the class," which must be set off by commas. There are multiple uses of commas in English: after introductory elements; between the two parts of a compound sentence; to separate items in a series; to set off parenthetical elements; and in quotations, dates, addresses, titles, and large numbers. Incidentally, one of the most common errors in student writing is misuse of commas, especially their overuse.
- End punctuation: End punctuation includes the period (.), the question mark (?), and the exclamation point (!). Declarative sentences, or those that make a statement about something, end with a period. So do imperative sentences, those which begin with a command, such as "Park your car across the street." A question mark follows an interrogative sentence, one that asks a question: "When will you be leaving?" An exclamation point ends a strong imperative sentence or an exclamation, such as "That's a really great idea!"
- Semicolon (;): The semicolon signals a stronger break than a comma. It separates independent clauses; precedes transitional phrases (conjunctive adverbs), such as *furthermore, otherwise, nevertheless, therefore,* and *however,* used between clauses; and separates items in a series when any of the items in the series contain commas (note that this sentence demonstrates the use of the semicolon to separate items in a series).
- Colon (:): The colon is generally used to direct attention to what follows, such as a list of items, for example, "Most important was what money represented: success, prestige, and power." It also follows the salutation of a letter and separates the hour and minutes in expressions of time.
- Dash (—): The dash is used to create separation. Two dashes often surround an interrupting phrase or idea in a sentence, or a dash may precede an explanation, for example, "Dahlias, geraniums, and fuchsias—those are my very favorite flowers." Writers of literary text often use dashes in creative and stylistic ways.
- Parentheses [(. . .)]: Parentheses are much like commas and dashes in that they are used to enclose elements that interrupt the flow of a sentence. They are always used in pairs. The material enclosed by parentheses includes an additional thought or related idea or some explanatory material

that is incidental to the sentence itself, for example, "The Smokehouse Restaurant (my favorite place to eat) has a great selection of hearty burgers to choose from."
- Hyphen (-): The hyphen is used to link parts of compound words, signals a break in a word that begins on one line and ends on the next, links prefixes with proper nouns (pro-American), links parts of nouns that include a prepositional phrase (attorney-at-law), and links the parts of fractions (two-thirds) and compound numbers (forty-six). I have found that most students are unable to distinguish between a hyphen and a dash, so you may want to emphasize the uses of each. A dash is longer than a hyphen; a hyphen is typed with one hyphen key on the keyboard, a dash with two (since there is no dash key on a typical keyboard). Autocorrect features will usually change a typed hyphen to a dash automatically.
- Apostrophe ('): The apostrophe shows the omission of letters in contractions; forms the plurals of letters, numbers, and symbols; and makes singular and plural nouns possessive, for example, "Jeremy's shoes," "the babies' room," "four $'s," and "couldn't."
- Quotation marks (". . ."): Quotation marks, like parentheses, also occur in pairs and enclose a word or group of words to separate them from the rest of the sentence, usually to show the exact words of a speaker. They also enclose titles of short works, such as stories or songs.

It is important in practicing close reading to read and use the punctuation marks provided by the writer, whether those marks are used in a creative way in literary text, such as with the cummings poem above, or when the punctuation follows standard English, because those marks are often the key to the meaning. Understanding the important role of punctuation is also useful in helping students improve their own writing because they need to understand the choices they have as writers. Punctuation is one of the very important "moves" that writers make.

Show students an example of an extremely long sentence, such as one of William Faulkner's characteristically lengthy and complex sentences, and have them analyze how the punctuation is used. Students can also analyze passages of informational text, observing the author's uses of punctuation and sentence structure. Gallagher (2015) provides an example to show how changing the punctuation can change meaning and style:

Sentence 1: If they ask, I will not do it.
Sentence 2: If they ask, I. Will. Not. Do. It! (p. 33)

What different effect is created by the punctuation used in the second sentence?

Let's examine a passage from Alice Walker's essay "In Search of Our Mothers' Gardens":

> For those grandmothers and mothers of ours were not Saints, but Artists; driven to a numb and bleeding madness by the springs of creativity in them for which there were no release. They were Creators, who lived lives of spiritual waste, because they were so rich in spirituality—which is the basis of Art—that the strain of enduring their unused and unwanted talent drove them insane. Throwing away this spirituality was their pathetic attempt to lighten the soul to a weight their work-worn, sexually abused bodies could bear. What did it mean for a black woman to be an artist in our grandmothers' time? In our great-grandmothers' day? It is a question with an answer cruel enough to stop the blood. (Walker, 2008, pp. 352–53)

(Excerpt from "In Search of Our Mothers' Gardens" from *In Search of Our Mothers' Gardens: A Womanist Prose* by Alice Walker. Copyright © 1974 by Alice Walker. Reprinted by permission of Houghton Mifflin Harcourt Publishing Company. All rights reserved.)

Consider how a variety of punctuation marks are used in this passage. If you were to use this passage with students, you might present them with the following guiding questions to use to help them analyze the use of punctuation:

1. What is the effect of the comma used in the very first line?
2. The use of the semicolon in the first paragraph is unusual. Walker could have just used a comma, but why does she choose to use a semicolon instead?
3. Why is the phrase "who lives in a spiritual waste" set off by commas, and does it need to be? Could it have been left out altogether?
4. Notice that the adjective phrase "which is the basis of Art" is set off by dashes. Why did Walker choose to use dashes here, and what effect does it create? Does it emphasize the idea or merely add additional information?
5. There are two compound adjectives at the end of the first paragraph. Why does Walker use a hyphen in one ("work-worn") and not the other ("sexually abused")?
6. The second paragraph uses two interrogative sentences (questions). What effect does asking these questions have? How does the second question add to the first? Does the second paragraph suggest that the answers to the questions will follow?

To make effective use of this strategy in the classroom, you can occasionally call attention to a specific passage of a common text and ask students to read closely and analyze and reflect upon the author's use of sentence structure and punctuation. These passages should be fairly brief. Use the strategy especially when a particular passage is very dense or complex. Have some discussion with students to help them understand how close reading involves slowing down and analyzing all the various "moves" the writer makes, including use of punctuation marks.

Strategy Five: Text Marking

Text marking can be a very powerful close-reading strategy. Some consider "margin notes" to be a separate strategy from text marking, but the term "text marking" here also refers to use of margin notes or annotation of text. Reading complex text requires students to use active reading, and text marking is a strategy that facilitates that active reading process by engaging students in doing something during their reading rather than just passively watching the words go by on the page. Annotation refers to jotting down notes to oneself in the margin during reading as well as underlining and highlighting of key information, terms, and ideas.

If students are unable to write on their copy of the text, have them do the text marking on sticky notes. Text marking is useful in helping students to achieve several of the objectives of the Common Core Reading Standards for both literary and informational text: read closely to determine what the text says explicitly, determine central ideas and themes, interpret words and phrases as they are used in the text, analyze the structure of texts, delineate and evaluate the argument and specific claims in a text, and read and comprehend complex literary and informational text. Adler and Van Doren (1972) identify the most commonly used marks of annotation: underlining of major points; using vertical lines, stars, asterisks, or other "doodads" in the margin to emphasize important statements; using numbers in the margin to indicate a sequence of points and numbers referring to other pages or parts of the text; circling key words and phrases; and writing in the margin or top or bottom of the page (cited in Frey & Fisher, 2013).

Berry (2014) presents a list of possible types of annotations students might use during their reading:

- For fictional or literary materials, have students identify elements of the author's style or use of literary techniques (foreshadowing, irony, metaphor, conflict, diction, etc.).
- Have students identify and make notes about the text features of the reading material.
- Ask students to use sticky notes to mark main ideas and supporting details.

- Ask students to use the five elements described in the section on margin notes: questioning, connecting, predicting, reviewing, evaluating.
- Ask students to write one-sentence summaries on every page.
- Ask students to write down key terminology and important words with definitions.
- Ask students to make notes about personal connections, how the text compares to other texts, to the student herself, or to the world.
- Have students make notes to trace the organizational pattern of the text.
- Have students make predictions about what will come next.
- Have students write down words or concepts they don't understand.
- Have students make comparisons, disagree with ideas, mark examples, mark analogies and comparisons, mark interesting or unusual facts.
- Have students mark good choice of words, images, or descriptive details. (pp. 66–67)

Follow this procedure for using text marking and annotation with your students:

1. Begin by assigning students an article, story, or piece of text, informational or literary. Preview the selection for students briefly.
2. Identify your purposes for having students read the text. What skills do you want them to demonstrate and what do you want them to notice and be able to identify during their reading. This will determine what types of text marking you want students to use during their reading. Use the list above, and choose the ones you want students to use during their reading. If you want them to identify only the main idea, supporting points, and critical vocabulary, then have them use highlighting, numbering, and circling of key words and terms. If you want them to use margin notes to reflect on their personal thoughts and reactions during their reading to make connections to the world outside of the text, then specify that. If you want them to write a brief summary statement at the end of each paragraph, then include that guideline in your directions.
3. Have students read the text and complete their text marking independently.
4. After students have finished, have them discuss their reading and how they used text marking with a partner.
5. Next, ask for a couple of student volunteers to allow their copy of the text to be displayed on the document camera. Discuss with the whole class the uses of text marking displayed in the student examples.
6. Finally, have students practice using this strategy frequently. After a while, it will become easier for students, and they will learn to use text marking automatically, as a natural part of their reading process.

Text marking is also a critical skill to help prepare students for college, where they will often be required to read difficult and complex text independently. The next strategy in this section describes a related strategy for close reading recommended by the AVID program, Charting the Text.

Strategy Six: Charting the Text

This strategy comes from the AVID program's Critical Reading materials (LeMaster, 2009) and is used here with permission from AVID Press of AVID Center, San Diego, California. The strategy is called Charting the Text: Analyzing the Micro-Structure, and it is a highly effective strategy for teaching students close reading of text, focusing on helping students distinguish between what an author is *saying* in a specific piece of text and what the author is *doing* in that text. Like several of the other strategies here, it moves students beyond merely focusing on the content of the text to focusing on the author's craft, "the deliberate choices authors make when constructing meaningful paragraphs" (LeMaster, 2009, p. 107).

LeMaster (2009) recommends using guiding questions, such as the following, to help students think about what the author is saying:

Saying

- What is the section about?
- What is the author saying?
- What is the content?
- What did I learn from the text?
- What information is being presented?

The following examples can help students analyze what the author is doing:

Doing

- Giving an example
- Interpreting data
- Sharing an anecdote
- Summarizing research
- Reflecting on a process
- Contrasting one idea to another
- Listing data (LeMaster, 2009)

Procedure for using this strategy:

1. Present students with their own copy of a passage from a piece of text or a short article.

2. Have students read the article carefully and use text marking during their reading. Have them read the article through twice, the first time focusing on what the author is *saying* and the second time, on what the author is *doing*.
3. Ask them to write their summary statements and charting statements in the margin as they are tracking what the author is saying and doing in the text. They might write summary statements about what the author is saying in the left-hand margin and chart statements about what the author is doing in the right-hand margin.
4. Another option is to hand out copies of the Charting the Text table (see figure 2.2). Ask students to use the table to chart their thinking about the text. As noted, if students are not able to use text marking on their text, they can use the table to record their charting statements, the left-hand column focusing on the *saying* and the right-hand column, on the *doing*.
5. Because the "doing" column can often be challenging for students, LeMaster (2009) also recommends providing students with a list of charting verbs, the words that indicate exactly what the author may be doing. He also recommends having students define for themselves each of these terms. They are divided into high-frequency verbs and medium-frequency verbs:

High-Frequency Verbs
Analyzing
Arguing
Asserting
Comparing
Contrasting
Connecting
Defining
Debating
Clarifying
Concluding
Discussing
Developing
Explaining
Extending
Illustrating
Interpreting
Listing
Offering

Proving
Questioning
Stating
Suggesting
Summarizing

Medium-Frequency Verbs
Acknowledging
Challenging
Compiling
Differentiating
Distinguishing
Establishing
Generalizing
Incorporating
Justifying
Predicting
Qualifying
Substantiating

Student Handout 8.1

Charting the Text Table: *Analyzing the Micro-Structure*

Use the table below or recreate this table to help organize your charting statements. Even though charting is most effective when done in the margins of texts, a table can be useful when distinguishing between what an author is *saying* and what an author is *doing*. It is also a good idea to use this table to chart texts that cannot be marked.

¶(s)	What is the author *saying* in the text?	What is the author *doing* in the text?
	Here are some questions you should ask: What is this section about? What is the content? What did I learn from this?	*Here are some examples of what authors do:* **Giving** an example **Interpreting** data **Sharing** an anecdote **Summarizing** information **Reflecting** on a process

Figure 2.2. Charting the Text Table
Source: Reprinted with permission from AVID Press of AVID Center, San Diego, California.

LeMaster (2009) provides some additional useful suggestions for the charting strategy:

- Explain to students that active reading becomes more important as texts become increasingly complex and more difficult to read.
- Assign readings that "vary in length, sophistication, and purpose" (p. 113).
- Provide students lots of time to practice the strategy and learn the associated skills.
- As students gain practice, they will become more proficient and faster with charting.
- Give students opportunities to talk about their experience with the text charting.
- Evaluate their ability to chart the text, and give constructive feedback. (LeMaster, 2009)

Like many of the strategies in this section, students need to have time to learn and practice the strategy. Use the strategy repeatedly so students can practice and polish their skills in active reading, which the charting strategy helps facilitate. You should have students master the text-marking strategy first, and then, once you are confident in their proficiency in text marking, have them move on to charting the text.

Strategy Seven: Interactive Shared Reading

Similar to the think-aloud strategy described earlier, the strategy called Interactive Shared Reading is a way of modeling for students how to read complex text. The strategy involves displaying a piece of complex text so that the reading is "shared" in the sense that the teacher reads the text aloud while students read silently (Fisher & Frey, 2013). Of course, students can also be asked to participate in the reading aloud of the text. If the text is displayed on a document camera or students are provided a copy of the text to write on, the teacher and class can focus on sharing responsibility for making meaning from the text, focusing on both content and author's craft, actively rather than passively. It is also advisable to do repeated readings of the passage to reinforce the skills of close reading and comprehending.

Fisher and Frey (2013) note that shared reading "allows the teacher to instruct through modeling by demonstrating how a skill or strategy is applied to a reading. After modeling, the teacher asks questions to foster discussion and provides prompts to scaffold students' understanding as they read text that is initially new to them" (p. 37). Much like the think aloud, this process helps students learn and develop the habits of good reading that they can begin to use independently.

To illustrate, let's take the opening passage from Ray Bradbury's 1953 novel, *Fahrenheit 451*. Students might be directed ahead of time to focus on a guiding question, such as "What clues are provided that help us to understand more about the main character?" The excerpt is followed by a scenario of how an interactive shared reading might unfold between a teacher and students:

> It was a pleasure to burn.
> It was a special pleasure to see things eaten, to see things blackened and changed. With the brass nozzle in his fists, with this great python spitting its venomous kerosene upon the world, the blood pounded in his head, and his hands were the hands of some amazing conductor playing all the symphonies of blazing and burning to bring down the tatters and charcoal ruins of history. With his symbolic helmet number 451 on his stolid head, and his eyes all orange flame with the thought of what came next, he flicked the igniter and the house jumped up in a gorging fire that burned the evening sky red and yellow and black. He strode in a swarm of fireflies. He wanted above all, like the old joke, to shove a marshmallow on a stick in the furnace, while the flapping pigeon-winged books died on the porch and lawn of the house. (Bradbury, 1953)

(Reprinted by permission of Don Congdon Associates, Inc. © 1953, renewed 1981 by Ray Bradbury.)

This excerpt is being told from the point of view of Montag, the main character in the story, whose job as a fireman is to burn books. Why does Montag find pleasure in burning things? He celebrates how he likes to see the fire eat up everything, blackening and changing things. The fire hoses are made of brass, and the author uses a metaphor of the nozzle as a "great python" that spits its venom, which is the kerosene. Another metaphor is used to describe Montag as "some amazing conductor playing all the symphonies of blazing and burning." Why does the author choose to use that metaphor of a conductor directing a symphony? What do the flames of a fire and the music of a symphony have in common?

The violence of the burning and destruction is portrayed in an almost poetic way. Fahrenheit 451 is the temperature at which paper burns (and also the title of the book), and the firemen wear the number on their helmets. Montag obviously loves his destructive work because his eyes shine with orange flame, much like the light of a fire, just thinking about flicking his igniter. The igniter turns on the fire hose. The author also uses personification when Montag flicks the igniter and the house "jumped up in a gorging fire." What does the word "gorging" mean? To gorge is to eat ravenously, just like the fire eats up everything in its flames. The fire is also described as burning the evening sky, creating bright colors of red, yellow, and black. When the narrator refers to fireflies, is he talking about actual fireflies or is he using a metaphor comparing the sparks from the burning fire to fireflies?

Montag enjoys setting the fire and watching it burn so much that he thinks about roasting a marshmallow on a stick, like one would do around a campfire. The ultimate goal of the fireman's work is to destroy all the books by burning them. The books as they catch fire are described with another metaphor, as flapping pigeons that burn and die on the porch and in the lawn of the house. The importance of destroying the books by fire is an important factor in this novel, as we will need to identify the reasons why this society is intent on destroying all books. This will get us closer to the theme of censorship and the question of why books and the knowledge they represent pose a threat to some people and societies.

Try this strategy with your class, using short pieces of text, especially those that are dense and somewhat challenging. Focus on your own reading of the text and ask students to contribute to an interactive process of meaning making as you read and examine the text together.

Strategy Eight: Monitoring Comprehension

This strategy and the next one (Multiple Readings) are critically important elements in helping students master close reading. Good readers monitor their comprehension and use active reading strategies. We must teach students strategies for monitoring their reading. Students are used to passive reading—that is reading something quickly, one time through, and not recognizing what they did or did not understand after their reading. Reading engages our brains in many different ways. Good readers are constantly asking themselves questions, extending their understanding, and making connections between the text they are reading and their own personal experiences. Good readers also visualize and create mental pictures while they are reading as well as make predictions about what the writer will do next or what will happen next in the narrative (Berry, 2014).

There are a number of good strategies to help students practice various facets of active reading, but the important point is that we want to teach students to monitor their own comprehension. We know that good readers recognize when they are not understanding something they are reading, and they adjust accordingly by re-reading, reviewing, paraphrasing, making connections, or even talking with someone else about the text. Whenever you ask students to read a piece of complex text, ask them to practice metacognition, or thinking about their thinking. Explain each of the following elements to students, and, if possible, give them examples of how you use them in your own reading, perhaps using a textbook chapter or reading selection from the class:

- Previewing the reading: Skim over the contents quickly, and notice text features, such as headings, captions, and visuals, and read first lines of paragraphs. Previewing should also involve examining the title for clues to the contents and noting any information about the author provided.
- Summarizing: Stop every few paragraphs to summarize what you have read so far, mentally or in written notes.
- Visualizing: Create mental pictures about the materials being read. Can you picture concepts the author is discussing or imagine what particular characters or settings look like?
- Making connections: Connect the information you are reading to what you already know, thinking about your prior knowledge and applying the concepts to something outside of the text.
- Asking questions: Think of questions that come to mind as you are reading the text, especially when information is confusing or hard to understand.
- Making comparisons: Compare the text to other things you have read, heard about, or learned previously. You can compare the text to similar pieces of writing and create analogies to other events and concepts.
- Re-reading: When you are not fully comprehending what you are reading, stop, go back a couple of paragraphs, and read the text a second time, trying to figure out what is making it hard for you to comprehend.
- Critical vocabulary: Identify important terminology or difficult words that you may not know the meaning of. If you cannot figure out the meaning of the word from the context, you may need to look it up. Vocabulary is especially important for texts in certain disciplines and technical subjects.

Use the graphic organizer provided here (figure 2.3) to remind students of what they should be doing mentally during their reading and to help them learn to monitor their comprehension.

Strategy Nine: Multiple Readings

We need to help students understand that during their years in secondary school and in college, an important element of academic reading is being able to read increasingly complex texts, many of which will be very challenging for students. Most students are used to reading something through one time only, preferably as quickly as possible. However, close reading generally requires multiple readings. Good readers make a habit of reading a specific article or

46   *Chapter Two*

STRATEGY	HOW I USED IT DURING READING	HOW DID IT HELP ME UNDERSTAND
Previewing the Reading		
Summarizing		
Visualizing		
Making Connections		
Asking Questions		
Making Comparisons		
Re-reading		
Critical Vocabulary		

Figure 2.3. Monitoring Your Comprehension

piece of text multiple times. These are usually not consecutive readings all the way through but instead a continual process of stopping, going back, and re-reading of particular sections.

If we compare reading to practicing any other type of skill, we will notice that the process is similar. If students are practicing playing a musical instrument, they will begin playing a piece of music, stop when they make a mistake, go back to the beginning, and try again. Or they will identify those places that are especially difficult and focus more closely on them by playing them over and over until they have mastered them. Providing students with this analogy is often helpful in making them understand that the same process must apply to reading. When good readers encounter challenging pieces of text, they slow down, go back, re-read, and try to figure out what is preventing them from understanding the content.

For middle and high school students, "multiple readings" means that they should read the text through *three times*:

- First reading: In this first reading, students should aim for basic comprehension. What is the central idea and basic meaning of the text? If the text is literary, what are some of the key elements of plot, setting, and character? If the text is informational, what is the central idea, thesis statement, and supporting details? For some students, they may also need to maneuver around challenging vocabulary or terminology. They may need more than one reading simply to gain a basic understanding of the text. Following the first reading, some teachers like to provide some scaffolding for students before asking them to do the second reading. This may involve providing some new information about the topic or the author or providing them with a target or focal point for their second reading, perhaps something you want them to look for, such as the author's use of details that create suspense or develop character.
- Second reading: The second reading should focus more on evaluating the text, noting the techniques the author used in writing the piece, how the piece is organized, and the author's uses of language. If the text is literary, you may want students to focus on the author's use of literary elements and techniques. If it is informational, you may want them to look for types of evidence, quality of evidence, supporting detail, and organizational patterns (cause-effect, comparison-contrast, description, definition, and so on).
- Third reading: By the time students approach the third reading, they should have a fairly strong understanding of the basic ideas in the text and the author's techniques. Now, we want to focus on having students extend their thinking about the text and its content, focusing on the broader themes and ideas. Have students complete the third reading while thinking about how the text may compare with other similar texts or pieces they have read. If students are reading a short story, for example, have them compare the story to other similar stories. Other stories may come to mind that have similar subject matter, themes, or techniques. They may identify a character from another piece of literature who is similar or think of other stories that also use flashback as a method of organization. For informational text, they may think of other articles or reading that has similar subject matter and ideas and make similar or opposing arguments. After this third reading,

we also want students to make some overall evaluation of how effective the text is and how well readers respond to it.

Following the third reading, have students engage in collaborative discussion or a post-reading activity that will help them combine their thinking with that of their peers to come to a deeper understanding of the text and its meaning.

Strategy Ten: Using Evidence from Text

The first Common Core Anchor Reading Standard (R1) requires students to "read closely to determine what the text says explicitly and to make logical inferences from it; cite specific textual evidence when writing or speaking to support conclusions drawn from the text." After students have read a particular piece of text, teachers often engage the class in discussion about the material read, but oftentimes, the discussion points are generalities based on impressions and overall response to the text. Students are not used to being asked to provide textual evidence to support their ideas and thinking. The ability to cite specific textual evidence is a key feature of the Common Core Standards and an important college-readiness skill. Teaching students to cite textual evidence requires a lot of modeling and much practice. Gradually, students will become used to providing specific evidence and identifying specific quotations from the text to support their thinking.

Model this strategy for the class at first. For the first few pieces of reading that students do as a whole class, use the two-column note format below, and complete it as a whole group so you can guide students and model for them how readers make inferences based on textual evidence. This modeling will also help provide scaffolding for students who will struggle with reading the text on their own. Strategies that provide modeling for students are especially helpful for students with special needs and English language learners, who may face a greater struggle with navigating complex text. Then provide students with simple pieces of reading at first, gradually working up to more complex text.

Provide students with a simple two-column graphic organizer, or have them use notebook paper to make their own two-column notes (see figure 2.4). This strategy can be used with literary or informational text. You might change the heading in the left column, depending on the genre of the reading assignment. You will also need to help students understand how readers draw inferences from text. An inference is a conclusion that we may draw based on our reading of the text, something not explicitly stated but that can be deduced. Explain the concept of making inferences to students by using an

Title of the Text:	Author:
Inference made about a character, setting, conflict, or theme, or other important element of the text.	Textual evidence (details, examples, quotes that support the inference)
1.	
2.	
3.	
4.	
5.	
6.	

Figure 2.4. Citing Evidence from Text

example, such as the following: "If the teacher walks into the classroom one day carrying a wet umbrella, what conclusion (inference) would you draw?" Give them a simple example of reading a short story in which a character exhibits a particular behavior. Based on the character's behavior, readers may draw an inference that the character is motivated by jealousy, infatuated with another character, depressed, and so on. The inferences we make are always based on some evidence, and the purpose of this strategy is to help them identify that evidence.

You may also want to require students to indicate specific page numbers or paragraph numbers where the specific textual evidence is located. At the end of this strategy, have students compare their two-column notes with a partner.

Strategy Eleven: Student-Determined Text-Dependent Questions

The Common Core State Standards place emphasis on the use of "text-dependent questions," the answers to which may be found in the text itself or may be inferred from the text, thus limiting the role of personal or text-to-self questions. As noted earlier, this focus on "staying within the four corners of the text" has been somewhat controversial because it limits the role of the reader and his or her own viewpoints and prior knowledge in creating meaning from text. It also effectively negates the idea that words on a page may have different meanings for different readers.

Beers and Probst (2013) express the concern that staying within the four corners of the page will translate into "teacher-dependent kids" in the sense that the teacher-created questions merely lead students to identify a predetermined answer to the meaning of the text. Perhaps the best solution is to ask students to generate their own questions as they are reading. The process of generating text-dependent questions necessitates use of close-reading strategies. Beers and Probst (2013) present a sequence of steps for guiding students in creating their own text-dependent questions. Here is the procedure they suggest:

1. Start with a short text that is complex and challenging.
2. Read the text aloud, with students following along.
3. Ask students to mark the spots in the text where they feel confused or have a question about something.
4. Have students re-read the selection. When they come to the passages they marked in the text, they should write a question about the text.
5. Next, as a whole class, compile on the whiteboard or poster paper all the questions that have been generated.
6. Next, have students work in pairs or small groups to think further about the questions they find most interesting or important. This step will encourage re-reading and finding evidence from the text.
7. Again as a whole class, discuss some of the most interesting questions, and ask students to share the ideas they came up with in pairs or groups.
8. As a follow-up, Beers and Probst (2013) suggest having students continue to answer the questions that were generated or work in small groups to analyze particular passages or write out answers to what they find to be the most interesting question.

Boyles (2013) also suggests that we encourage students to ask questions and suggests using the following questions as examples to help teach students the kinds of questions they can ask:

- Who is speaking in the passage?
- Who seems to be the main audience?
- What is the first thing that jumps out at me?
- What is the next thing I notice? How are the ideas connected?
- What seems important here?
- What does the author mean by _____?
- Is the author trying to convince me of something?
- Is there something missing from this passage that I expected to find?
- Is there anything that could have been explained more thoroughly?
- Is there a message or main idea?
- How does this sentence or passage fit into the text as a whole?

Boyles (2013) notes that becoming a good reader means reading "with the eye of the writer," which involves analysis of the writer's craft—consideration of how the text is written. Teaching students about the various methods writers use is key to helping them develop the skills of close readers (as discussed earlier in Strategy Four).

Another approach to questioning the text is to ask students to try writing questions during their reading that relate to three different categories, each building up to a deeper level of reading:

- Main ideas and details: These are questions that require locating and citing specific information from the text and, in some cases, making inferences about it.
- Craft and structure: These are questions that require the reader to analyze how the author developed the text and what text structures are used (refer also to the next strategy in this chapter regarding text structures). This also involves analyzing the author's word choices and use of language.
- Integrating ideas: These questions involve evaluating a text, perhaps comparing it with another text, making judgments about the ideas and arguments used in the text, and thinking critically about the content.

Another option would be to ask students to write questions that address various levels of Bloom's Taxonomy (Knowledge, Comprehension, Application, Analysis, Synthesis, and Evaluation).

Imagine how this strategy of having students create text-dependent questions might work with a piece of complex text in your classroom. Perhaps it is a passage from a difficult essay or editorial on a controversial or complex topic, or perhaps it is a challenging piece of literary text, such as a passage from a novel or a Shakespearean sonnet. This strategy can be an effective one because, first of all, students are determining what's important and challenging in the text. Also, they are engaging in multiple reading of the text, and they are making meaning from the text collaboratively.

Suppose your class is reading this excerpt from *The Federalist*, No. 2, by John Jay. Have them work with partners to practice the suggestions presented and create a few questions they can ask as they read the passage. Then have students share their questions with another pair or in small groups:

> To the people of the State of New York:
> When the people of America reflect that they are now called upon to decide a question, which, in its consequences, must prove one of the most important that ever engaged their attention, the propriety of their taking a very comprehensive, as well as a very serious, view of it, will be evident. Nothing is more certain that the indispensable necessity of government, and it is equally undeniable, that whenever and however it is instituted, the people must cede to it some of their natural rights in order to vest it with requisite powers. It is well worthy of consideration therefore, whether it would conduce more to the interest of the people of America that they should, to all general purposes, be one nation, under one federal government, or that they should divide themselves into separate confederacies, and give to the head of each the same kind of powers which they are advised to place in one national government.
> It has until lately been a received and uncontradicted opinion that the prosperity of the people of America depended on their continuing firmly united, and the wishes, prayers, and efforts of our best and wisest citizens have been constantly directed to that object. But politicians now appear, who insist that this opinion is erroneous, and that instead of looking for safety and happiness in union, we ought to seek it in a division of the States into distinct confederacies or sovereignties. However extraordinary this new doctrine may appear, it nevertheless has its advocates; and certain characters who were much opposed to it formerly, are at present of the number. Whatever may be the arguments or inducements which have wrought this change in the sentiments and declarations of these gentlemen, it certainly would not be wise in the people at large to adopt these new political tenets without being fully convinced that they are founded in truth and sound policy. (Jay, 1787)

Strategy Twelve: Teaching Text Structure

This strategy focuses on close reading of informational text. To help students learn to comprehend complex text, we need to teach them to recognize common text structures and organizational patterns that different texts may use.

Understanding the text structure is often a key to understanding the content. All of these patterns are frequently used in textbooks that students are assigned to read, yet students often are unable to identify the organizational structure the author is using, which inhibits their comprehension of the text. There are several common text structure or patterns of organization that we must teach students about, with some examples provided for each:

- Description: Text that is primarily focused on providing information and descriptive detail about an event, person, place, or concept. Examples: a *National Geographic* article that focuses on the people and culture of a specific country or region in the world or an encyclopedia article about an important historical figure and his or her contributions.
- Chronological or sequential: Text that presents a series of events that are told in time order. Of course, chronological structure is normally used to structure narrative text, but it can be used for various types of informational text as well. Examples: a set of directions for how to change the oil in your lawnmower that presents the steps in the process, a chapter from a history textbook that recounts the sequence of events leading up to the entrance of the United States into World War II, or a plot summary for a novel.
- Comparison-contrast: This is text that shows the similarities and differences between two or more subjects. The subjects could be people, objects, places, time periods, or actions. Comparison-contrast may be structured in a point-by-point fashion, where the two subjects are compared according to a series of criteria, or they may be organized in a one-side-at-a-time fashion, where one of the two subjects is discussed in the first part of the piece and the other subject in the second part. Examples: a comparison of two different athletes from the same or different sports, a comparison of two civil rights leaders and their influence, or a comparison of two scientific theories that focuses on their similarities and differences.
- Cause and effect: This is a type of text that explains why something happens by identifying the causes. It explores how the causes and effects are related to each other, shows how events may lead to other events, and shows how a single event may have several causes or several effects. Examples: an essay that discusses the causes of the Civil War, an editorial that explores the likely effects of carbon emissions and their role in climate change, or a textbook chapter that explains the causes and effects of volcanic activity.
- Concept-definition: This type of text focuses on explaining and defining a concept. Any concept or idea that is somewhat complex or controversial may require concept definition. Often, this type of writing is called "extended definition" or "expanded definition." Examples: an article that

defines the concept of *entropy*, an article that defines the concept of *energy*, an essay that defines the concept of *heroism*, a science textbook section that defines the concept of *propulsion*, or an excerpt from a math textbook that defines *ordinal numbers*.
- Problem-solution: This type of text describes a problem and presents one or more possible solutions. Sometimes, this type of text also starts with a problem, then identifies the causes of the problem, and then proposes a solution. Examples: a magazine article describing the problem of poaching of wild animals in Africa and exploring possible solutions, a scientific paper exploring possible solutions to the problem of endangered species, an economics text that discusses possible solutions to an economic recession, or an informational document that informs people what can be done in the event of a natural disaster in their area.

It's important to note that not every text falls into one of these categories exclusively. Writers often rely on more than one organizational structure to accomplish their rhetorical goals. In some texts, one section may follow a single organizational structure, while another section will make use of a different structure.

You may be wondering how to help students understand and recognize these various text structures. First, collect some examples of various articles and pieces of informational text, perhaps some magazine articles, editorials, and encyclopedia articles on various topics. Over time, you will have gathered some examples of all the above types of organizational structures. Teach students about one type of text structure per week. After six weeks, students will have been introduced to all six common types.

From then on, whenever students read a piece of informational text, have them identify the organizational structure or structures, and spend some time discussing how and why the author organized the article in that way. You can also have students practice by working in pairs. Hand each pair a different article, and ask them to read it and identify the organizational structure used. Then have them pass their article on to another pair for their analysis.

Strategy Thirteen: Color Coding of Text

Color coding can be used in a variety of ways. For this strategy, you will need to provide students with individual copies of the text they will be reading. You will also need a supply of colored pencils, enough so that each student can have several different colors. This strategy is rather self-explanatory: students will be looking for certain aspects or features of the text and marking them with a particular color-coding system using colored pencils. Students will also have to provide the coding key (to show what each color represents). This strategy can be used with various types of text. It can also be used in teaching essay writing by having students analyze and color code sample essays. For example, you might ask them to identify the thesis statement with one color; supporting reasons with another; specific details and examples with a third; and transitions with a fourth.

Begin by considering what type of text students will be reading, and identify your purpose and goals for having students read the text. The elements students will color code should be the elements that you want them to be able to recognize and identify: main ideas, details, technical terms or unfamiliar vocabulary, specific examples, statistics, use of authorities, quotations from source material, transitional words and phrases, statements of opinion versus statements of fact, or specific literary elements, such as figurative language or imagery.

Suppose in an honors English course, students need practice in preparing for the International Baccalaureate exam, where they will have to independently read and analyze a challenging piece of literature. Your goal for students is to give them practice so they can read and analyze complex literary text independently. One of the strategies you might use to meet this goal is color coding, which will allow students to demonstrate that they can identify particular literary elements and techniques. Let's say you have asked students to read and color code Henry Wadsworth Longfellow's poem "Mezzo Cammin":

Mezzo Cammin
Written at Boppard on the Rhine,
August 25, 1842, just before leaving for home

Half of my life is gone, and I have let
The years slip from me and have not fulfilled
The aspirations of my youth, to build
Some tower of song with lofty parapet.
   Not indolence, nor pleasure, nor the fret
   Of restless passions that would not be stilled,
But sorrow, and a care that almost killed,
   Kept me from what I may accomplish yet;
   Though, half-way up the hill, I see the Past
Lying beneath me with its sounds and sights,—
   A city in the twilight dim and vast,
   With smoking roofs, soft bells, and gleaming lights,—
And hear above me on the autumnal blast
The cataract of Death far thundering from the heights.

First, direct students to read this poem through a minimum of three times, quickly the first time and then slowly and deliberately the second and third readings. Then assign them to use five different colors to mark the following elements in the poem:

- Words and phrases that create strong images
- Words and phrases that point to motifs and themes
- Rhyming words (they will need four different colors to track the four rhymes in the poem)
- Shifts in patterns, ideas, or tone
- Examples of figurative language

The color coding is the tool that students use to engage in close reading and analysis of the text. You can follow this up by having them write a brief analysis or commentary on the poem in which they share their thinking about the author's use of literary techniques and how they relate to the overall ideas and themes of the poem.

Strategy Fourteen: Commentary

Some schools are International Baccalaureate High Schools. International Baccalaureate is an advanced educational program that follows the requirements of the International Baccalaureate Organization (IBO) and allows students who meet the requirements to graduate with an International Baccalaureate Diploma (and potentially earn college credit based on their test scores in various subject areas). In some schools, such as the one where I teach, students take Pre-IB English during freshman and sophomore years and IB English junior and senior years.

One of the requirements of the IB English program is that students will be able to complete both oral and written "commentaries." The requirements of the commentary fit perfectly with a discussion of close-reading because the commentary is used with a piece of (usually literary) text, and it requires students to focus on a small portion of the text, practice close-reading strategies, and analyze the techniques the author is using. The commentary focuses on why writers make the particular choices they do and the effect those choices have on the reader. The commentary allows students to learn how to focus on the craft and structure of text, which is the focus of Common Core Reading Standards 4, 5, and 6. In their commentaries, students must analyze the author's word choices and identify how they shape the meaning and tone; they must analyze the structure of the text and how the parts relate to the whole; and they must analyze not merely content but also *style*.

Our Pre-IB students are required to learn the techniques of commentary and complete several written and oral commentaries during the year. A commentary is simply a specific type of essay, a form of literary criticism. Even though our Pre-IB and IB students are honors-level students, all students can benefit from learning the techniques of the commentary to improve their ability to closely read and analyze text. In writing commentaries, they have to decide what is important about the text and what they want to focus on. Their commentary must focus on one or more literary elements the author uses and absolutely must focus on the effect of the author's stylistic choices. What is the effect on the reader? Commentaries can be taught in various ways, but here is one possible procedure:

1. Begin by assigning a piece of text. For the IB exams in English, our students are presented with a piece of literary text that is unfamiliar to them, and they must analyze the text in a limited time period and be ready to deliver their commentary. For classroom purposes, allow students to choose a piece of text from a particular author or among a given set of works. If you are teaching a longer piece of text, a short story or novel, students will need to choose a brief excerpt, a "snippet" of the text they want to focus on. For poetry, you can give students a number of different poems and allow them to choose one for their commentary. If a particular poem is long, they will want to focus on only one particular section or a few lines from the poem. For example, during our study of Walt Whitman's poetry, students can choose either one of the short Whitman poems or one section or snippet from a much longer poem, such as "Song of Myself." Ask students to choose a passage that strikes them as interesting or stands out to them in some way as a starting point.
2. Provide students with a list of common literary terms that they may want to use as they are preparing their commentary, reminding them that a good commentary must focus on literary elements and techniques, not merely personal reactions and thoughts. A possible list might include the following: figurative language, simile, metaphor, personification, imagery, theme, motif, symbol, foreshadowing, irony, satire, flashback, point of view, conflict, tone, setting, protagonist, antagonist, mood, denotation, and connotation.
3. Next, students need to carefully read the passage several times, taking notes and thinking about the author's techniques. It's a good idea to have them use the text-marking strategy during their study of the piece.
4. Next, students should start writing down their thoughts and impressions as they read and think about the passage: What questions does it raise? What feelings does it create? What makes an impression on them? What

powerful images and words are used? Next, students must ask how the author achieves the particular effect that the piece creates. The essential question is, how? The "how" question addresses the craft of fiction: how it is created and what the effect is. This is where students must begin to examine the language and techniques the writer uses: diction, figurative language, imagery, tone, point of view, and elements of style and, if the passage is poetry, poetic elements, such as rhyme scheme, rhythm, line length, and so forth.
5. Next, students will need to pull together all their ideas into a coherent essay about the piece. They should first write a thesis statement that sums up the overall impact of the passage and captures the "argument" they want to make about the passage. While their commentary must focus in particular on the brief excerpt or snippet they have chosen, they can also relate the snippet to the larger text and its themes.
6. Next, students should write a "central assertion," the overall main idea (much like a thesis statement) that their paper will provide evidence for. They should also write a brief scratch outline of the various aspects and elements of the text they want to discuss.
7. Next, students begin writing the commentary. The first paragraph should quote the excerpt or snippet in its entirety and include their central assertion. Before you ask students to write their first commentary, use models of written commentaries provided by the IB program and also commentaries written by previous students. Providing models of good commentaries is critical to helping students successfully write their own. It is also critical that students understand they must refer directly to the text, use quoted lines and phrases, and provide specific detail that shows what techniques the author is using and their effect upon the reader. You may need to practice this process with students and show them how to correctly incorporate quoted phrases, lines, and passages into their own writing.
8. Ask students to bring to class a rough draft of their commentary on the day it is due, and have them share it with a partner or small group. Students can often give very helpful advice and suggestions for how to improve the commentaries of their peers. Students then take their commentaries home or to the computer lab, revise them, and submit the final copies.

You can score the commentaries on a scale of 1 to 5 in four areas:

- Understanding of subject: understands major ideas and shows an ability to interpret them, understands and explains major stylistic devices of the author and their effect.
- Quality of ideas: original ideas, meaningful critical comments, appropriate and justified personal reaction to the text.

- Presentation: the commentary is clear and organized, ideas are developed in a purposeful sequence.
- Formal use of language: correct use of grammar, spelling, sentence structure; effective word choice and voice; and use of language appropriate to the commentary.

Scores of 5 are exceptional; 4, strong; 3, developing; 2, weak; and 1, very weak.

While the commentary is a specialized form of literary criticism required of advanced-level students, the basic elements of the commentary can be used by all teachers to help students build skills in close reading. Even if you don't require students to write a full commentary, you can still teach them how to engage in the close analysis of a text that the commentary requires: identifying the techniques the author uses, examining word choices, analyzing the structure of a text, and identifying why the author makes the choices that he or she does and what effect those choices have on the reader.

Often, rather than having students write a complete, essay-length commentary, you can ask them to write a "mini-commentary," which is actually more like a quick write, where they focus on a specific piece of text and analyze the elements and techniques used in a brief period of ten or fifteen minutes during class. This is a technique that can easily be incorporated into any ELA class or other content-area classes.

Strategy Fifteen: Analyzing a Source

An important college readiness skill, and one that Common Core focuses heavily on, is reading and interpreting information from source material. We need to give students lots of practice in close reading of passages of informational text. In writing courses, you can use articles and editorials collected from various places. These articles should be about a variety of topics, especially ones that would be interesting and relevant for teenagers and also those that will stretch them in their reading ability. Create a file of articles, either in hard copy or electronic form, that you can use to help students practice close reading. You might use articles from news magazines, newspaper editorials, and online articles. CNN.com and MSN.com are good sources of articles as well as the websites of major newspapers, such as the *New York Times*.

If you teach in an AVID school, you also have access to AVID weekly articles (www.avidweekly.org). AVID stands for "advancement via individual determination;" it is an excellent college preparation program that helps to prepare students for success in four-year colleges. Your school's AVID site coordinator can provide you with a user name and password to access these great articles. New articles are updated to the site regularly. Another good source of articles is the library databases your school or district likely subscribes to. The Gale Databases contain the Opposing Viewpoints database, an excellent source for controversial topics and current issues, with articles that present both sides of the controversy.

Use the procedure here to help students' practice analyzing source material:

1. Locate a newspaper or magazine article or an editorial on a current issue, one that expresses an opinion.
2. Have students preview the article by looking at the title and making a guess about the contents of the article. If available, have them also look at brief information about the author and his or her qualifications, experience, and expertise.
3. Have students read through the article, using the text-marking strategy, making margin notes, underlining key points, and circling any unfamiliar words or terminology. After the first reading, have students use their smartphones or a dictionary to look up definitions of any unfamiliar words.
4. Have students read the article a second time to identify the main idea, thesis, or claim of the article and also to make a list of five or six key points the article makes. Here are some questions students can ask themselves as they are analyzing the article:

- What is the main idea or claim of the article?
- What are the supporting reasons or support for the claim?
- How are the ideas in the text related to each other?
- What specific examples and evidence does the author use?
- What is the author's conclusion?

5. Next, have students extend their understanding of the article by having them either participate in small-group discussions or do a piece of writing on the topic. For writing classes, you might require students to write full-page journal entries for each article they read. The journal articles should include a brief summary, but most importantly, provide the students' responses to and evaluation of the article and its argument. The articles serve as a springboard for students' own journal entries but also help them practice close reading and analysis of complex text. Students can then discuss and share some of their ideas they captured in writing. You could also have students write a more formal essay that analyzes the source, focusing on the techniques the author uses to build the argument and how useful the source is for information on that specific topic.

After students have become more comfortable with reading and analyzing articles, start using multiple pieces on the same topic; for example, you might choose two articles that present opposing viewpoints about a controversial issue. Using multiple articles requires students to learn to synthesize ideas from several different sources in their writing.

Strategy Sixteen: Paraphrasing

Whenever you are teaching research writing, always spend some time teaching students how to take notes in paraphrase form because much of the source material in their paper will need to be in their own words. While paraphrasing is a writing activity, it also requires students to engage in very close reading of the text, and therefore, it is an effective strategy for teaching close reading. A paraphrase is a restatement of the original material that retains all of the original ideas but in the writer's own words. It is similar to a summary but is more detailed (summaries are usually written in a very condensed form and are much shorter than the original text). When students do note taking from source material, and when they are asked to answer questions about a piece of text, they often resort to copying wording directly from the original source, which is of course not acceptable in formal writing.

If readers truly understand the content of a passage, they can restate the ideas in their own words. Paraphrasing requires changing the language and sentence structure so that you have expressed the original idea of the passage in your own words. It is actually much more challenging than one might imagine. Paraphrasing requires students to notice the details of a passage and truly understand the meaning and author's intent in order to restate the ideas in their own words. It also requires maintaining the tone and point of view of the original.

Try writing (or orally reciting) a paraphrase of the following passage from a *Time* magazine article about the opening of diplomatic relations with Cuba:

> Will engaging Cuba change how it's governed? That's far less certain. The example of China, another country that remains communist in name, demonstrates that economic reform doesn't automatically mean political freedom. The most prominent dissidents inside Cuba now say they welcome the opening, and the State Department cautiously notes that political detentions there dropped to 178 in January, from a monthly average last year of 741. But any new tolerance is as untested as the fragile spirit of cooperation between Havana and Washington. The nominal enemies are clearly pulling together to create a political environment hopeful enough that members of Congress feel they can vote to roll back the embargo. (Vick, 2015, p. 39)

How did you do? Are you confident that you expressed all the ideas from the original passage in your own words and did not copy any wording from the original? You probably noticed that you had to read and re-read the passage carefully to make sure you understood the ideas in the original.

To teach students how to write a paraphrase, follow these steps:

1. Start by clearly explaining what a paraphrase is: Paraphrasing means more than just changing a few words here and there. A paraphrase is a restatement of the original ideas in your own words. Be very careful to adequately paraphrase so you are not unintentionally plagiarizing from your source. Do not copy exact wording from the source. Go through the original passage and pick out one idea at a time, and then state that idea in your own words.
2. Show students a couple of examples of original passages, followed by a paraphrase of the original. Most writing handbooks include examples of passages that have been paraphrased. Some also give examples of unacceptable paraphrases versus those that are well-paraphrased versions.
3. Present students with a short piece of text, probably no more than one hundred words or so. Starting with informational text may be best to help students practice this process. However, you can also use the paraphrase activity with challenging literary material, such as poetry and passages from Shakespeare. Ask students to read through the passage a couple of times. Highlighting key words and terms might also be useful.
4. Next, have students write their own paraphrase of the original passage. Here are some tips for writing a good paraphrase:

    - Refer to the author or give a source citation at the very beginning.
    - It is okay to retain some of the key words or terms from the original, but use synonyms wherever possible.
    - Rewrite each idea in the passage in your own words. Don't copy exact wording or sentence patterns.
    - Delete needless words, and be sure to use your own words and phrases to state the ideas.

5. When students have finished writing their paraphrase, ask for a couple of volunteers to share their work by reading their paraphrase aloud or displaying it on the document camera. Then have students exchange their paraphrase with a partner, and have each pair check the paraphrases to verify that all the original ideas are included, that the meaning expressed in the paraphrase is the same as in the original, and that the paraphrase is stated in the writer's own words.

6. Come back to the paraphrase activity frequently to give students opportunity to practice this process and better learn to engage in close reading of complex text.

Strategy Seventeen: KNOWS

For students to engage in close reading of complex text, the new knowledge they are reading about needs to be connected to their prior knowledge and understanding of the topic and concepts associated with it. One way for teachers to aid students in this process is to use the acronym KNOWS:

- K—Knowledge and experience of the students (prior knowledge)
- N—New knowledge: New information that can be gained from the text
- O—Organizing the new knowledge and understanding and integrating it with their prior knowledge
- W—Widening their knowledge, which may include connections to additional sources or reading material or application of the new knowledge
- S—Sharing of knowledge

When using the KNOWS strategy with students, follow this procedure. Let's assume students are assigned to read a passage from Henry David Thoreau's famous essay "Civil Disobedience."

1. First, ask some simple questions about students' prior knowledge regarding the concept of civil disobedience: "What do you think that term means?" "Is it okay to break the law if the law is wrong?" "Can you think of examples of people who have challenged authority or refused to follow the law as a form of protest or to bring attention to a specific issue or problem?" "Would you be willing to go to jail to take a stand or do what you believe is right?"
2. Move on to the N. Give students a purpose and focus for their reading. Read the essay "Civil Disobedience" to find out how Thoreau defines "civil disobedience." Identify his reasons for protesting the U.S. government's role in the Mexican-American War.
3. Next comes the O. Have students do some form of note taking as they are reading, using two-column notes, Cornell Notes, or a graphic organizer of some sort, such as a concept map. This helps them to organize and make sense of the complicated ideas they may be encountering in the text.
4. For the W, provide some other resources, perhaps a short film or video or another piece of writing. You might use another excerpt from Thoreau's writing or a passage from another writer that expresses similar themes.

You might ask them to read a short excerpt from Martin Luther King and compare civil disobedience with King's notion of nonviolent protest. Students could also make connections to modern-day civil rights protesters who stage protests and rallies and sometimes run into conflict with local authorities. For the W section, you want to help students apply the information to a wider context and make connections to the modern world.

5. Last comes the S, where students are asked to share their knowledge. This can be done during a whole-class discussion, small-group discussions, partner discussions, or sharing of their notes or graphic organizers or in a short piece of reflection writing about what they have learned. The sharing process gives students a chance to solidify their thinking about the issues and adds to their understanding and retention as well.

Strategy Eighteen: Apps to Promote Reading Skills

It is possible that the use of digital devices could actually promote students' reading skills in several ways. We should capitalize on the use of technology whenever possible to encourage close reading and comprehension. A research study conducted in Canada, the United States, and Australia found that young students' interactions during the reading process occurred on "both a physical and cognitive plane of meaning making" (Simpson, Walsh, & Rowsell, 2013, p. 123). They found that the sense of touch that students use during interactions with iPads aided them in making meaning from the text, as did the use of hyperlinks and nonlinear pathways that computers allow, for both reading and writing (Simpson et al., 2013).

More schools and classrooms now provide access to computer labs and sets of computers, such as Chromebooks, made available in individual classrooms. We should make use of media and technology in whatever ways we can to help cultivate literacy learning. This section presents several potentially useful apps that you could recommend and use with students. Most of our students now own smartphones, and for those who do not, they could possibly access similar programs in online versions. Here are some potentially useful apps, some of which are designed for test preparation (SAT), some for improving reading skill and speed, and some for accessing and downloading audiobooks. The apps discussed here are free apps, although others are available for a small fee:

- Accelerated Speed Reading Trainer: This app automatically tracks users' reading progress each time they take a speed test. It measures a starting point, allows users to select a performance goal, and generates a personalized training program. After completion of ten lessons, the system measures reading improvement. Users read a passage, select "done" when finished, and then answer a few questions about the content. It is designed to promote both reading speed and comprehension. When taking the initial test, I read 395 words per minute and "already demonstrate some advanced reading techniques" (as expected). The system works on strengthening eye muscles, reducing subvocalizing, and increasing the reader's capacity to absorb more information at once. Flashcards are used to train the eye to read all the words at once rather than moving left to right. It also uses a built-in column highlighter that quickly flashes across three columns on the screen to increase reading speed. Another speed-reading app called OUTREAD Speedreading is also available for $2.99.

- NEWSELA online and in app format provides news and nonfiction reading geared to particular reading levels. Users can sign in to this program with a Google account and then set up a profile as a teacher or student. The teacher can set up classes in the system and provide students with a class link. The system can also be linked to Google Classroom. It provides a code by class, and the teacher can then invite students to join. The app provides numerous articles, and users can search for articles by subject. If you'd like to take a look at this app without joining, you can also browse the reading materials first. It includes individual articles as well as text sets on various topics. For example, if you search for text sets for the Cold War, you will find four. For the topic of immigration, there are seven text sets. NEWSELA is a potentially very useful and rich source of nonfiction reading materials that teachers and students can easily access.
- SAT Prep by Ready 4 SAT: The test prep materials for the PSAT, SAT, ACT, and others are very useful for improving students' reading skills since all of these tests cover reading comprehension, writing, sentence structure, conventions, and so on. This app allows students to study and build skills in the topics covered on the SAT, using their phone. Students can create their own personalized SAT course. With this app, students can easily practice their close-reading and comprehension skills while also preparing for the SAT.
- Prep 4 SAT Reading: This is an app, similar to the previous one, that allows students to practice skills specifically tested by the reading/writing sections of the SAT. They work on skills such as sentence completion, identifying errors, reading comprehension, and improving sentence and paragraph structures.
- Audiobooks—Classics for Free: We can perhaps use digital technology to encourage students to read by making audiobooks available to them on their phones. This app allows students to search for popular books by title, author, and ratings. It includes genres such as biography and autobiography and science fiction. It includes several classic novels and Shakespeare

plays. The authors available, however, appear to be mostly white and male (Doyle, Stoker, Dickens, Wells, London, Austen, Verne, Twain, and Wilde). The app provides reviews/summaries of each book and allows users to download and listen.
- Books—23,469 Classics to Go: This one is similar to the previous audiobooks app. It includes a wider array of genres, however: adventure, drama, fantasy, history, humor, mystery, poetry, politics, science fiction, and thrillers.
- College Reading Comprehension: This app is an excellent resource to help students practice and improve their reading comprehension skills. It includes lessons and practice activities for strengthening reading comprehension, focusing on skills critical to close reading, such as previewing, contextualizing, summarizing, identifying purpose, engaging with the text, re-reading, and being selective. It also features several common reading strategies, such as RTR (Read, Think, Repeat), SQ3R, SOAPS, THIEVES, and others. The practice sections provide reading material by topic, such as entertainment, travel, health and nutrition, and technology. For example, for an article on health and nutrition, the segment asks students to use the highlighter tool to highlight specific examples of superfoods during reading and then take a quiz to test their knowledge.
- There are several other apps that you may find useful and want to recommend for students. For example, one is called "Me Studying: Reading for College Success." This one, however, costs $4.99. Other apps, like Goodreads, may help students find interesting and motivating reading material. Most major magazines now come with an app version as well, so students might identify some magazines relevant to their interests and download the app so they can do some reading on their phones.

Strategy Nineteen: The One-Pager

The one-pager is an engaging and creative activity that helps students build skills in close reading, helping them visualize and conceptualize what they have read. The one-pager is an AVID strategy that comes from the *Write Path* strand of the AVID curriculum materials. The strategy asks students to create a single page containing their written and graphic interpretation of the reading assignment. The words and images students choose to include can be both literal and symbolic. Following are the guidelines for students' one-pagers:

1. Use a single sheet of 8-1/2" by 11" unlined paper.
2. The entire page must be filled.
3. Written work must be in ink or typed.

4. Use as much color as possible, unless black and white is more appropriate for the theme or mood of the text.
5. All of the following items must be included:

   - Title and author of the work.
   - Three or more excerpts or passages from the reading that are important for some reason.
   - A personal response to each passage chosen (summary or interpretation).
   - One or more graphic representations, which could be pictures or graphics related to the text or passage, illustrative or interpretive.

6. Include a border or some other decoration on the page.
7. When finished, one-pagers should be posted on the wall, and students must be prepared to give an oral "tour" or explanation of the one-pager (*The Write Path*, 2012).

The one-pager is a great activity not only for the fact that it asks students to exercise some creativity but also because it asks them to determine what the key ideas and themes of a particular piece of text are and to present those in a concise format. The strategy allows students to demonstrate their close-reading skills and share their understanding of the text. It is also appealing to students who are more visual learners. This section presents two variations for the original one-pager activity, one for literary text and one for informational text, because you may want to be able to use the strategy with a number of different types of texts and for different courses. Figure 2.5 shows one approach to the one-pager for literary text, and figure 2.6 presents the one-pager for nonfiction or informational text. Both include a scoring rubric for the finished products.

My students recently completed the one-pager for literary text based on their reading of Fitzgerald's novel *The Great Gatsby*. Figure 2.7 presents Ana's one-pager, and figure 2.8 presents Shelby's. Unfortunately, the reprinted versions here do not allow you to see the original color used by the students.

Instructions for the One-Pager (for literature)

A one-pager is a written and graphic representation on a single sheet of paper of a particular poem, story, novel chapter or a particular section of a piece of literature. It may be a literal or symbolic representation of the piece (or both). The One-Pager will help you visualize and better understand what you have read.

Directions:

1. Use a sheet of plain, white (8 ½" X 11") paper. Place your name and period number on the back.
2. The one-pager you create must fill the entire page.
3. The text and written work that you include on the page must be in ink or typed (no pencil).
4. You should use color as much as possible (unless black and white is more appropriate or matches the mood of the piece).
5. Include all of the following parts arranged on the page in any way you choose:
    a. Title and author of the piece (as well as chapter or section number)
    b. Two or more short quotations or excerpts from the reading
    c. A personal response, summary, interpretation, or theme statement
    d. One or more graphic representations which might include illustrations/drawings, magazine pictures, clip art, computer-generated graphics, photographs, or other images that are related to the piece of literature. Be creative!
    e. Place a border on the page and any other decoration that you wish to add.
6. When you have finished, hang your one-pager on the classroom wall. Be prepared to explain your one-pager to your classmates.

Scoring rubric:

Includes the author and title	5 points
Includes two or more significant quotes:	5 points
Include a response, summary, interpretation	5 points
Include symbolic and meaningful graphic representations	10 points
Is thoughtful, well-written, colorful, and creative with border	5 points
	30 Total points

Figure 2.5. The One-Pager for Literature

Instructions for the One-Pager (for nonfiction)

A one-pager is a written and graphic representation on a single sheet of paper of a particular essay, article or piece of informational text. It may be a literal or symbolic representation of the piece (or both). The One-Pager will help you visualize and better understand what you have read.

Directions:

1. Use a sheet of plain, white (8 ½" X 11") paper. Place your name and period number on the back.
2. The one-pager you create must fill the entire page
3. The text and written work that you include on the page must be in ink or typed (no pencil).
4. You should use color as much as possible (unless black and white is more appropriate or matches the mood of the piece).
5. Include all of the following parts arranged on the page in any way you choose:
   a. Title and author of the essay/article.
   b. Two short quotations or excerpts from the reading that are significant and meaningful.
   c. A statement of the purpose of the text: why was the article/essay written?
   d. A statement of the main idea/thesis/claim.
   e. An example of a special technique that the author uses (figurative language, parallelism, tone, satire, specialized terminology, allusions, listing, humor, examples (real, hypothetical/extended), word choice, etc.). This could count as one of your quotes.
   f. One or more graphic representations, which might include illustrations/drawings, magazine pictures, clip art, computer-generated graphics, photographs, or other images that are related to the piece of literature. Be creative!
   g. Place a border on the page and any other decoration that you wish to add.
6. When you have finished, hang your one-pager on the classroom wall or around the room. Be prepared to explain your one-pager to your classmates.

Scoring rubric:

Includes the author and title	5 points
Includes two or more significant quotes:	5 points
Include a response, summary, interpretation	5 points
Include symbolic and meaningful graphic representations	10 points
Is thoughtful, well-written, colorful, and creative with border	5 points
	30 Total points

Figure 2.6. The One-Pager for Nonfiction

Figure 2.7. Ana's One-Pager
Student work reprinted with permission.

Figure 2.8. Shelby's One-Pager
Student work reprinted with permission.

Chapter Three

Textual Evidence and Elaboration

TEXTUAL EVIDENCE: WHAT IT IS AND WHY IT'S IMPORTANT

An important element of both reading and writing is the ability to identify and cite textual evidence (and in writing, to elaborate on that evidence). The CCSS for Literacy place high importance on identifying and using textual evidence, most explicitly in Reading Standard 1. For example, looking at the Grade 9–10 band for Reading Literature and Informational Text, Standard 1 specifies "Cite strong and thorough textual evidence to support analysis of what the text says explicitly." This clearly states that when students read a text, they must be able to draw conclusions and inferences from it and base those conclusions on "strong and thorough" textual evidence. Many of the other standards also depend on students' ability to identify textual evidence, so it is important for us to explicitly teach this skill.

The Writing Standards also place importance on use of textual evidence. For example, Writing Standard 1 requires students to write arguments "using valid reasoning and relevant and sufficient evidence." Certainly, one of the ways that most teachers evaluate a student's written argument is on the strength of the evidence provided in support of the argument.

The subpoints for Writing Standard 1 specify that the argument must develop claims and counterclaims fairly, "supplying evidence for each" in addition to pointing out strengths and weaknesses of the argument. Writing Standard 2, which addresses informative/explanatory writing, does not specifically use the term "textual evidence" (we tend to think of evidence largely in the context of argument writing), but it does specify that students will be able to "develop the topic with well-chosen, relevant and sufficient facts, extended definitions, concrete details, quotations, and other information or examples" (W2b).

Writing Standard 3, which addresses narrative writing, replaces textual evidence with "effective technique, well-chosen details, and well-structured event sequences." Writing Standard 8 also addresses the use of evidence in the context of conducting research; it specifies "Gather relevant information from multiple authoritative print and digital sources" and also notes the importance of integrating this information effectively into writing. Finally, Writing Standard 9 comes back to textual evidence, specifying "evidence from literary or informational texts to support analysis, reflection and research."

It is certainly important for teachers to help students build the skills of identifying relevant evidence, recognizing the different types of evidence, and citing specific evidence to support conclusions and inferences, whether in speaking or in writing. It seems that too often in classrooms, during discussion especially, teachers accept generic statements of interpretation based on reading of a common class text. These statements are often open-ended impressions and generalities that we may not require students to provide evidence for. To build the skills involved in using textual evidence, we must start expecting students to cite specific evidence from the text, whatever form that evidence takes. It's good to ask students to identify and refer to a specific passage, line, or statement from the text that supports their interpretation.

The tendency to tolerate generality is especially true in reading and discussion of literary text, where much is often left to an individual reader's interpretation. For many literary texts, it is certainly true they can be interpreted in multiple ways, but rather than just allowing students to offer their general impressions and feelings about the selection, we need to ask them to specify and elaborate on their evidence for the conclusion they draw.

For example, if students are reading and discussing Salinger's *Catcher in the Rye*, you might ask them to think about what emotional and psychological problems the main character, Holden Caulfield, may be suffering from. Rather than general comments, such as "Holden seems to be confused" or "Holden seems to be depressed," require that they cite specific evidence, examples and quotations from the text that led them to that conclusion. As the authors of Common Core state, students must be able to make "nontrivial inferences beyond what is explicitly stated in the text regarding what logically follows from the evidence in the text" (Coleman & Pimentel, 2012, p. 7).

Even the Common Core Speaking and Listening Standards for Grades 9–10 specify drawing on evidence from text (SL1a) as well as evaluating a speaker's use of evidence and the credibility and accuracy of sources. Students are also expected to provide supporting evidence in presenting their ideas in speaking, discussion, and digital media presentations. Whether or not your state and district require you teach to Common Core Standards, the ability to identify and elaborate on textual evidence and generate good textual evidence for their own writing is an important skill, one that students will need to become proficient in academic writing. It is a critically important college-readiness skill. The Common Core's focus on use of evidence will lead to stronger writing instruction in our classrooms.

The Revised Publishers' Criteria for the Common Core also sheds some light on the matter of textual evidence: "At the heart of these criteria are instructions for shifting the focus of literacy instruction to center on careful examination of the text itself. . . . The standards focus on students reading closely to draw evidence and knowledge from the text" (Coleman & Pimentel, 2012, p. 1). The Publishers' Criteria later refers to careful attention to specific passages in the text during reading. Thus, the call for "text-dependent questions" that focus on helping students in "gathering evidence, knowledge, and insight from what they read" and, further, that the tasks students are asked to complete "should require careful scrutiny of the text and specific references to evidence from the text itself to support responses" (Coleman & Pimentel, 2012, pp. 6–7).

So what does the term "textual evidence" mean, and what does such evidence consist of? Essentially, the concept of evidence comes from rhetoric, the art of persuasion. It is the factual or anecdotal evidence, or reasons, that an author selects to illustrate his or her ideas and provide support for the claim or argument. Textual evidence applies not only to arguments, however; in any type of writing, authors have a responsibility to provide adequate supporting detail and evidence to support their points. If you are writing a comparison-contrast essay for two different types of vacation destinations, you would still need to select lots of specific details and examples to provide evidence for your points of comparison. There are several types of textual evidence. In academic writing contexts, writers usually rely on four basic types of evidence:

- References to specific examples, incidents, and details from the text
- Summaries of information from source material
- Paraphrases, close restatements of the ideas in source material
- Quotations, or using exact words, phrases, or passages from a text. Authors can cite specific words or phrases, include brief quotes of a few sentences, or include longer quoted passages.

However, there are other types of things we might also consider evidence. Evidence, more simply, is anything that helps lead us to a conclusion. Even in speaking and conversation, we provide textual evidence for our assertions. If you are having a conversation with a friend about a book you recently read and you make the assertion that it is one of the greatest books of all time, you will likely go on to explain your reasons for why you say that and provide specific details or examples that support your reasoning as well as why you were able to personally connect with the book.

So, although we may primarily use the four types of evidence above in academic writing, writers actually depend on other types of textual evidence as well, including factual information and statistics, information from source material (citations), quotations, personal experience and observations, personal testimony of experts or eyewitnesses, anecdotes, and even analogies and allusions.

For those of you who are teaching Common Core, the SBA and PARCC tests both expect students to not only identify an author's claim but also to identify the writer's supporting evidence, which may be stated explicitly or implicitly. Students are also expected to be able to make valid inferences, and they need to use the evidence from the text to support their inferences. However, in writing, it is not enough to simply cite textual evidence; students must also elaborate on the evidence. If a quote or example is used as evidence, the student must explain what the quote or example shows or illustrates and how it serves as evidence to support the claim. The evidence must be integrated into the student's writing, must be relevant, and must be specific.

The SBA argument-writing rubric, for example, states that students must use a variety of elaborative techniques in order to score well. However, it does not define elaborative techniques except to note that relevant personal experiences can be used as an elaborative technique. Elaboration of evidence suggests not just the inclusion of evidence but also discussion and explanation of it; for example, it may mean providing a source citation and then using an example to explain and illustrate.

SIMPLE WAYS TO TEACH TEXTUAL EVIDENCE

Here are some simple techniques you can incorporate into your everyday instruction to explicitly teach students how to identify, analyze, and use evidence from text:

- In the course of reading and discussion of a wide variety of types of texts, get into the habit of frequently asking the question "How do you know?" This simple question prompts students to identify the evidence that supports their conclusion or assertion. In the earlier example of *Catcher in the Rye*, when a student attempts to "diagnose" Holden Caulfield, she might say, "I think Holden suffers from posttraumatic stress disorder." You could then ask, "How do you know?" The student might respond in a number of

ways: by quoting a particular passage from the text, giving examples of specific incidents and details from the text, summarizing an episode, or citing a number of different statements or quotes from Holden. In short, she would be providing textual evidence to support her theory.
- Use multiple readings. Emphasize with students the importance of reading the text through the first time just to get a general sense of the piece of text and then going back a second time to read more carefully, analyze the text, and think about the author's use of specific evidence. In class, point out specific passages that are important, and ask students to take a few minutes to re-read that section.
- Anytime you ask students to read something, provide them with a purpose for reading. What do you want them to look for? For example, "As you read this article, I want you to notice how the author references certain research studies and information from experts in the field to provide support for his point. Be ready to give at least three different examples" or "As you read this short story, I want you to analyze the methods of characterization the author uses."
- While not all writers find outlines useful, it is a good idea to have students create an outline for their paper that states their claim and includes the specific pieces of support they will use to provide textual evidence. For example, if students are writing an essay on the theme of race and identity in *Huckleberry Finn,* you could have them state their claim and then identify and write down in outline form specific pieces of support for the claim: specific incidents, examples and quotations from the story, and quotes and ideas from other secondary sources about the novel.
- Many of the strategies presented in the previous section on close reading also provide help in building students' skills in using textual evidence. Consider using the think aloud from Chapter Two to model specifically how a reader would analyze evidence presented in a piece of writing. If students are reading an article about the effects of climate change, you would ask, "How does the author prove his point that climate change is having several negative effects on the environment and weather conditions?" Students might then answer, "One thing he does is provide specific examples of extreme weather conditions that have never been seen before. He also cites testimony from scientific studies and gives quotations from experts." Also, the text-marking strategy is useful in helping students identify textual evidence. You can even ask students to use a specific mark or symbol in the margin to identify types of textual evidence the author is providing. Paraphrasing is also useful because it requires students to state the author's argument and evidence in their own words.
- Every week or so, identify an article from your collection of articles and editorials that you will ask students to read. Help them polish their reading comprehension skills by asking them to read the article independently, write

out a statement of the author's claim, and then write a list of the evidence and support provided for the claim. You need to stress with students that sometimes authors will state the claim directly, usually somewhere near the beginning of the article, but other times, the claim may be only implied or suggested, not directly stated. In some articles, the claim may not be stated until closer to the end. As an extension of this activity, after students have become proficient in identifying claim and support, have them write a brief paragraph that evaluates the author's use of evidence, thinking about the quality of the evidence the author provides, how convincing it is, and perhaps identifying what other pieces of support the author might have used.

- Use small collaborative group discussions to have students practice identifying evidence from text. Using a specific article or brief passage from a piece of literature, have the group draw a conclusion or make an assertion about the text and then discuss the specific evidence and details from the text that support their conclusion or inference.

SAMPLE STRATEGIES

A group of colleagues at our school, who all collaborate in a professional learning community, realized in the course of evaluating our students' writing that students were having trouble using an appropriate level of specific evidence to develop their claims (during sophomore year, our students focus on argument writing). For our honors students, it was more a matter of adequate elaboration of the evidence that was problematic. For example, we noticed that most students were proficient in providing a quotation from the text but often failed to provide elaboration, explanation, and discussion of the quote and what it illustrates.

The SBA rubric for argument writing specifies "The response provides thorough and convincing support/evidence for the argument(s) and claim that includes the use of sources" and "effective use of a variety of elaborative techniques" (which may also include personal experiences). After brainstorming, the group designed useful strategies to help our students master this skill. Special thanks to Cara Fortey and Matthew Isom, who participated in designing these activities.

Color-Coding Strategy

The team decided to use sample argument essays and have students color code them to help build skills in identifying an author's techniques and use of evidence. Since students were working on learning how to write effective arguments, we used a sample argument essay and asked students to color code it. You can use this activity with any argument essay. Figure 3.1 shows the assignment sheet with student directions. You will also want to provide students with a list of common transitions and a large supply of colored pencils. You can find lists of common transitional words and phrases in writing handbooks, and there are several of them available online as well. We used a list of transitions specific to argumentative writing.

Poetry Explication: Supporting Your Reading by Citing Textual Evidence

The group of colleagues wanted to help students with identifying and citing textual evidence not only in argument essays and informational text but also in literary selections. This is especially important for our IB students because they will be expected to complete commentaries for pieces of literary text. As noted in Chapter Two, the commentary requires close reading in addition to use of evidence provided in the text and elaboration of that evidence to support their interpretation. My colleague, Matthew Isom, designed this poetry

---

Argument Writing Color Coding Activity

Standard: W1: Write arguments to support claims in an analysis of substantive topics or texts, using valid reasoning and relevant and sufficient evidence

W1a: Introduce precise claim(s), distinguish the claim(s) from alternate or opposing claims, and create an organization that establishes clear relationships among claim(s), counterclaims, reasons, and evidence.

W1c: Use words, phrases, and clauses to link the major sections of the text, create cohesion, and clarify the relationships between claim(s) and reasons, between reasons and evidence, and between claim(s) and counterclaims.

Directions:
1. First study the list of transitional words and phrases for argument writing provided.
2. Choose three different colored pencils and write the colors here:
    Color 1: _____
    Color 2: _____
    Color 3: _____
3. Read the argument essay provided.
4. Read the essay a second time, using your colored pencils to mark the essay as follows:
    Color 1: claim or thesis statement and restatement of the claim in the conclusion.
    Color 2: supporting points and specific pieces of evidence used in the body of the essay
    Color 3: transitional words, phrases, or sentences used throughout the essay
5. When you are finished, work with your partner to compare your color-coded versions. Check to be sure that you and your partner have identified the correct thesis statement and evidence, and marked all the transitional devices.

Figure 3.1. Argument-Writing Color-Coding Activity

Poetry Explication Activity
Supporting Your Reading of a Poem by Citing Textual Evidence

Assignment: Choose one of the poems we are studying and write a two-page typed explication discussing the point the author is making. Discuss the "hand of the artist" and how the author uses literary devices and other techniques to make the point. Remember, all you have are black letters on a page, and from that, a work of art with a message is created. Your job is to explain how.

Although most people use the word "interpretation" when they talk of finding the meaning of a work of literature, I prefer the word "explication" because when you explicate something, you find textual support to back up your interpretation, and you then explain what the words of the poem mean. When we speak of "elaboration of evidence" in writing, we are talking about explaining how examples (words) lead you to your interpretation. Good writing is all about elaborating upon evidence to fully convince the reader that you have nailed your interpretation. Interestingly, if you do a thorough job, your interpretation must be considered even by those who disagree with you because you will have used the author's own words to make your point.

To explicate is to explain the meaning of something by analyzing the ways that the words, images, and other details of the poem work together to create its meaning. To do this you:

1. Find the theme (sometimes finding the single most important line or even word will be very beneficial).
2. Determine how specific words, images, sounds of the poem, and so forth, help you understand this theme.
3. Write your interpretation showing that your interpretation is backed up by the words of the passage. You will need to refer to at least three specific examples from the text, which you will quote and analyze.

Before you begin writing, you will need to color mark the poem for at least three different literary elements. You will hand in your color-marked poem stapled to your paper. To color mark a poem, use colored pencils to mark the use of the following literary elements (at least three):

Imagery
References to nature
References to time
References to color
Word connotations
The sound effects of the poem
Alliteration
Repetition of words and concepts
Rhyme
Metaphor
Symbolism
Punctuation
Allusions
Psychological states

For example, you might analyze:
1. The sound (lyrical, choppy); you might look for contrasts and underline each reference in its own color
2. Imagery (light and dark, harsh versus peaceful)
3. Thematic contrasts (life and death, hope and despair)

As you are marking, it is vital that you ask yourself this question:
What is the effect? --Why did the author use these specific words?
Your written explication will focus on the way the author used the words to create the theme. After color marking, re-evaluate the theme, perhaps revise it, and then start writing your explication focusing on the theme. Be sure to discuss how the words and other parts you marked create the meaning of the poem. If you do this well, anyone who reads your paper will have to agree, at least to some extent, with your interpretation, because you will have shown that the very words of the poet state what you claim is the point or message of the poem.

Figure 3.2. Poetry Explication Activity

explication activity, which has been somewhat modified here (see figure 3.2). This explication activity can be used with any type of poem.

Figure 3.3 is a modification of Mr. Isom's poetry explication activity for use with a specific poem: Walt Whitman's "O Captain! My Captain."

Using Transitions

One of the things our team had noticed in students' argument essays was that they had slightly lower scores in the category of organization. Many students

---

Poetry Explication

"O Captain! My Captain" by Walt Whitman

O Captain! my Captain, our fearful trip is done,
The ship has weather'd every rack, the prize we sought is won,
The port is near, the bells I hear, the people all exulting,
While follow eyes the steady keel, the vessel grim and daring;
    But O heart! heart! heart!
      O the bleeding drops of red,
        Where on the deck my Captain lies,
          Fallen cold and dead.

O Captain! my Captain! rise up and hear the bells;
Rise up--for you the flag is flung--for you the bugle trills,
For you bouquets and ribbon'd wreaths--for you the shores a-crowding,
For you they call, the swaying mass, their eager faces turning;
    Here Captain! dear father!
      The arm beneath your head!
        It is some dream that on the deck,
          You've fallen cold and dead.

My Captain does not answer, his lips are pale and still,
My father does not feel my arm, he has no pulse nor will,
The ship is anchor'd safe and sound, its voyage closed and done,
From fearful trip the victor ship comes in with object won;
    Exult O shores and ring O bells!
      But I with mournful tread,
        Walk the deck my Captain lies,
          Fallen Cold and Dead.

Explication Assignment:
Write an explication of the poem, analyzing the words, images, and other literary devices of the poem and how they work together to create its meaning.
1. Start by identifying the main idea or theme of the poem.
2. Determine how the specific words, images and sounds of the poem help you understand the theme.
3. Write an interpretation of two to four paragraphs in which you elaborate upon the evidence (explain how examples and details lead you to your evidence). In other words, don't just quote words or lines from the poem, but explain what they mean and what their effect is upon the reader.

Figure 3.3. **Whitman Explication**

need to be taught how to effectively organize their writing, and of course, transitional words and phrases are an important aspect of organization. You can use several different methods to teach students how to use transitions; the important thing is that you do make it a point to deliberately teach transitions. This will improve the organization of students' essays and enhance their use of elaborative techniques. Transitional words and phrases help students develop their ideas and encourage them to elaborate on their evidence with further ideas and explanation. One way to introduce transitions is to teach students about the various categories of transitional words and phrases, such as the following:

- To make addition: *likewise, moreover, in addition, we can also see that, to further strengthen the argument, it is important to note that*
- To show agreement: *since, because of, in light of this fact, to say nothing of, similarly, of course, as a matter of fact*
- To show contradiction: *although this may be true, nevertheless, however, despite, on the other hand, on the contrary, admittedly*
- To show cause-effect and consequence: *due to, in order to, to fully understand, by the same token, although this may be true*
- To give an example/illustrate: *given that, under these circumstances, certainly, therefore, for this reason, since, it is important to realize, for example, whenever, because, the most compelling evidence, a point often overlooked, to put it another way, in other words, because*
- To show effect or result: *consequently, therefore, since, for this reason, as a result*
- To signal conclusion: *in conclusion, in the final analysis, as a result, in either case, in essence, given these points*

You may think of additional transitional expressions to add to this list. You can find lists of common transitions in any writing handbook and online. When students are working on a draft, have them use this list or a similar one and require them to use and identify a certain number of transitional words and phrases in their papers, maybe a minimum of five. Have them highlight the transitions in their draft or identify them in the margins.

Another activity can be used to help students analyze how writers use transitional words and phrases to create coherence in an essay. Since a writer's use of transitions helps link the claims and evidence together and hold the parts of the essay together, this activity is also useful for teaching students how writers elaborate on their evidence. After completing this exercise, students were asked to evaluate and revise their use of transitions in their own essay drafts. The following activity includes two examples of essays, ones that use a variety of transitions. All the transitional words and phrases were removed and placed at the top of the page. Students were assigned to correctly place the transitions into the right spot in the essays.

Although our students were working specifically on argument writing, neither of the essays here is an argument essay. One is an expository essay (process), and the other is a personal narrative. Since transitions are used in all types of writing, the particular mode of the sample essays was not necessarily important for accomplishing the goal of increasing students' awareness of how transitions work. Figure 3.4 presents the using transitions activity.

Students struggled with this activity. It is challenging to identify the correct transitions, and many students noticed that some transitions, particularly with the first essay, could be used interchangeably. Therefore, the activity is a good starting point for a discussion about the role of transitional devices and how various transitions serve different purposes. Figure 3.5 shows the answer key for this activity.

Using Transitions

Directions: The following essay is called "Hosting a Summertime Patio Party." The transitional words and phrases have been removed from the essay. Using the list of removed transitions below, insert them back into the essay in the correct places:

Transitions:
Also
Generally
One
One way
Depending on
One of
Another
In general
Over the years
Of course
Another method
As far as
Another
When
Also
One of
After
Also

Figure 3.4. Using Transitions Acitivity

Essay:
        I have always loved summertime, especially summertime patio parties and barbeques that I often host at my home. _____ I have discovered there are three essential elements to creating a successful summer patio party: creating a festive and fun atmosphere, including choosing my guests carefully, preparing lots of delicious fresh food, and providing some interesting forms of entertainment.

        _____ creating a festive atmosphere is concerned, there are a number of simple and effective ways to do this. _____ is by carefully selecting guests I know will like each other and are likely to have a good time together. _____, it's important to make sure that the guests I invite are compatible and share some common interests. At my patio parties, you can always guarantee there will be lots of spirited conversation, and a fun and relaxing atmosphere. _____ the day chosen and the particular occasion, it is _____ possible to add some decorations, such as brightly colored streamers on the patio. I also set up kerosene lanterns or tiki torches around the perimeter of the patio to create a warm atmosphere and also provide a source of light. If we are celebrating a birthday, Fourth of July, or some other special occasion, I will make sure to have a cake, some fireworks, or some other appropriate festive additions.

        My very favorite part of summertime entertaining is preparing lots of great food my guests will enjoy. I love to cook and often spend two days prior to the barbecue event preparing food items such as fresh salads and side dishes. _____ the easiest types of food to prepare for a patio party is hamburgers and hotdogs that can be cooked on the grill. I always set up a serving table somewhere on the patio where I can lay out all the side dishes and condiments that my guests can easily access. The table may have green salads, fresh vegetable trays, cheese plates, deviled eggs, baked beans, chips and salsa, and, if I am serving burgers or sausages, lots of condiments such as pickles, mustard, relishes, ketchup, and fresh toppings. Soda, punch, and other beverages will be provided on the serving table. For some occasions, we may _____ choose some wine, a festive bowl of punch, or a selection of teas and coffee. I enjoy preparing different types of foods and various items that can be cooked on the grill. _____ of my specialties is barbecued ribs. _____combination I enjoy cooking on the grill are steaks and seafood, perhaps a nice piece of salmon or some fresh oysters. This type of main dish can be combined with some fresh vegetables, sliced potatoes, or corn on the cob also cooked on the grill.

        _____ I have established a festive atmosphere and provided some delicious food, I make sure that my guests will have some form of entertainment for our patio event. There are lots of great options for entertainment. _____ I host a barbecue, I try to think of a couple of board games that guests will enjoy, a game of croquet, or perhaps a fun Twister contest in the yard. _____, most guests will simply enjoy some good conversation and good music playing in the background. _____, fireworks always work well and, since we have a small pool, I make sure it is available for guests who want to take a swim as well. _____ my guests will do whatever they want to enjoy themselves, relax, and have a good time.

        My patio events and summertime barbecues almost always turn out to be a success. How do I know? _____ I check to make sure I have created a fun and festive atmosphere, have provided lots of delicious food, and that my guests are finding ways of entertaining themselves and each other, relaxing and having a good time.

        _____ of determining whether my summer barbecues are a success is to ask

Figure 3.4. *(continued)*

the many friends and neighbors I have invited over the years. They will tell you that they are always guaranteed to have wonderful food and a fun time at my patio parties.

Part II:

Directions: The following essay is called "A Story of Love and Loss." The transitional words and phrases have been removed from the essay. Using the list of removed transitions below, insert them back into the essay in the correct places.

Transitions:
Where I had once been the only child left at home
Most importantly
After my classes ended
By doing this
From the moment
In the last year of my mother's life
Each morning before going to class
As I move on with my life
However
Also
As my mother's condition deteriorated
There
With this compassion
Although
Now
By the spring of my sophomore year

Essay:

      Twenty years ago, I was born into a loving family with two doting parents and two protective older siblings. I was the youngest child, and the baby of my devoted parents and grandparents. My older brother and sister grew up and moved away to live their own lives, and my parents grew apart as the years went by. They eventually divorced but remained on friendly terms and made sure I was provided for in every way. _____ they were no longer married, my parents always did whatever was necessary to make sure I was cared for in the best possible way and provided with everything I might need to be successful and happy. I loved both of them dearly and recognized and appreciated how hard they worked to raise me and my older siblings. My childhood years were filled with trips to the beach, camping and hiking adventures, and lots of educational sightseeing trips. I was protected and sheltered somewhat through my younger years, but I eventually grew up, graduated from high school, and entered college, looking forward to lots of intellectual opportunities and a bright future. Everything changed suddenly and without warning during my freshman year of college. My parents sat me down one day and told me that my mother was terminally ill with cancer.

      _____ my parents decided to tell me, I was overwhelmed with a barrage of confusing emotions and tremendous fear. Losing one of my parents so early was not something I

Figure 3.4. *(continued)*

had ever anticipated or even considered, and it completely changed my outlook and attitude. Because my brother and sister were much older, I had always been very carefree and independent, more like an only child: _____, this time I did not have time to fully comprehend what was happening and was incredulous over my mother's fateful diagnosis. They have waited to tell me about her illness until they were certain that her condition was terminal. My responsibilities were now great and overwhelming. Over the next year, I helped to take care of her. _____, I was now playing the parent role as I watched my mother's condition deteriorate.

_____, I had made some significant changes in my own life; _____ and she became gradually more sick, she depended more on me for much of her everyday care.

_____ I took her to the treatment center where she was able to receive chemotherapy and radiation to combat the cancer that was slowly eating away at her. _____, I would rush home and try to focus on my studies and coursework so that I could visit my mother again later in the day. _____ I prepared nutritious foods, cleaned up her house and made sure she was taking all of the oral medications that had become necessary as her pain increased. I found that I learned a lot about various treatments and medications as well as much of the terminology that the medical experts used. It was late at night by the time I arrived home to my room, too tired to do anything else but fall into bed exhausted. I felt great grief and sympathy as I watched my mother's struggles, admiring the courage and fortitude she displayed every day, and fought back tears as I tried to comfort her when she was so sick she could barely get out of bed. I _____ saw her fear and it began to affect my life as well, as we both knew that the end was near for her.

My mother died, on August 15, 2013. _____, I recognized that I had been grateful to have made the sacrifices that I did to take care of my mother in her last days and weeks. She _____ taught me about strength and courage, and how we never know where life will take us. _____, she helped me to gain a sense of compassion and strength that I would never have otherwise learned. I also discovered how powerful was my ability to love even in the face of great loss. I felt compassion not only for my mother, but for everyone in the world around me, a caring sense of empathy and a desire to help. I am thankful for my mother's life, grateful for all the years she guided me, and grateful for her love, which will never die. She told me in her final days how much she loved me and how much she appreciated all I had done for her, as I also did for all she had given to me. _____ comes an even greater responsibility. Annie Johnson Flint wrote "God hath not promised skies always blue, flower-strewn pathways all our lives through; God hath not promised sun without rain, joy without sorrow, peace without pain." My struggle throughout this ordeal was to learn patience, strength, and compassion. _____, it is my hope that my suffering teaches me a greater sense of appreciation for life's beauty, and an awareness of its vulnerability and lack of certainty. _____, I will be able to show great compassion and understanding for others who, like me, have loved and lost.

Figure 3.4. *(continued)*

```
                    Answer Key for Transitions Activity
"Hosting a Summertime Patio Party"
1. Over the years
2. As far as
3. One way
4. Also
5. Depending on
6. Also
7. One of
8. Also
9. One of
10. Another
11. After
12. When
13. Generally
14. Of course
15. In general,
16. One
17. Another method

"A Story of Love and Loss"
1. Although
2. From the moment
3. however
4. Where I had once been the only child left at home
5. By the spring of my sophomore year
6. As my mother's condition deteriorated
7. Each morning before going to class
8. After my classes ended
9. There
10. Also
11. In the last year of my mother's life
12. Most importantly
13. By doing this
14. With this compassion
15. As I move on with my life
16. Now
```

Figure 3.5. Answer Key for Transitions Activity

A Time to Dig Deeper: Answering Text-Based Questions

Another strategy for helping students identify textual evidence comes from *Common Core Literacy Lesson Plans: Ready to Use Resources, 9–12*, edited by Lauren Davis (2013). It is called "A Time to Dig Deeper: Answering Text-Based Questions." This strategy focuses on asking and answering text-based questions. The authors recommend Anna Quindlen's essay "A Quilt of the Country" as a focal text, but any other piece of complex text could be used as well. Quindlen's essay was published September 26, 2001, in *Newsweek* magazine. You can easily access it online. The objectives for this strategy are that students will read an informational essay and answer text-based questions about it as well as analyze what the text says explicitly, make inferences, and determine where the text leaves matters uncertain, all objectives that are clearly addressed in CCSS Reading Standards.

Here is a procedure to follow, as recommended by Davis (2013):

1. Present copies of the essay to students. Ask students to brainstorm what they know about quilts and discuss what the title "A Quilt of the Country" might mean. Call students' attention to the date the article was published, September 26, 2001.
2. Have students read the article independently, encouraging them to use active reading strategies, such as margin notes and identifying unfamiliar words.
3. Next, have students follow along as you read the essay aloud.
4. During a whole-class discussion, ask students a series of text-based questions that will require students to return to the text and identify words, phrases, and paragraphs in order to provide an answer. These might include questions such as Why did the author use this phrase? Why did the author emphasize this point? How did the author illustrate or defend her point? How does the word choice create a particular tone or mood? Which details reveal the theme of the piece? Here are some recommended questions:

   - How does Quindlen compare the qualities of the United States to those of a quilt?
   - What does the author mean by "mongrel nation" in the second sentence, and why does she return to it in the next-to-last sentence?
   - Why does the author say, "You know the answer" at the end of the third paragraph?
   - What does the author mean when she says people were concerned that "the left side of the hyphen—African-American, Mexican-American, Irish-American—would overwhelm the right?
   - What can you infer about the author's childhood and parents' neighborhood?
   - What questions does the text raise but not answer?

If you are using a different piece of text, use the questions here as a model to write your own text-based questions for students.

5. Have students work in pairs to complete the handout (figure 3.6). Practice this strategy with several pieces of text. Then, after they have had lots of practice, as an extension activity, have students write text-based questions of their own based on a piece of informational text. Remind students that text-based questions require close reading of the text and attention to specific words, details, paragraphs, and sections of the text, focusing on the ideas in the text rather than personal opinions and judgments based on one's own experience.

The next chapter will provide examples of specific performance tasks designed for commonly taught pieces of literature, which you can use in your classroom if teaching the particular works. You can also use them as models to create your own performance tasks designed around a common theme or piece of text.

Answering a Text-Based Question Step-by-Step

1. Write the question that you were asked to answer.

2. Underline key words in the question that will help you focus your response. For example, does the question ask why, ask you to compare two things, or include a quotation from the text?

3. Reread the text. As you do, list words, phrases, sentences, and/or ideas in the text that can help you answer the question:
   -
   -
   -
   -

4. Think about how the evidence you gathered in step 3 can help you answer the question. Which pieces of evidence are strongest? Which link most logically to the question? Place checkmarks next to the strongest pieces of evidence.

5. Write your response to the question using the strongest pieces of evidence. Be sure to link each piece of evidence to the question; don't just quote words randomly. Does the evidence help explain a metaphor? Does it provide a reason that supports the author's key idea? Does it help show how the author created a certain effect, such as a tone toward the topic or a mood in the reader? Identify this connection clearly for your reader.

Figure 3.6. Answering a Text-Based Question Step by Step
Source: Republished with permission of Taylor and Francis Group LLC Books, from *Common Core Literacy Lesson Plans: Ready-to-use Resources, 9–12*, edited by Lauren Davis, 2013; permission conveyed through Copyright Clearance Center, Inc.

Chapter Four

Performance Tasks Designed for Specific Literary Texts

WHAT ARE PERFORMANCE TASKS?

This chapter presents several specific performance tasks designed for novels and other literary selections commonly taught in schools. So what is a "performance task"? McTigue's (2015) definition of a performance task is a "learning activity or assessment that asks students to perform to demonstrate their knowledge, understanding, and proficiency" (p. 1). In other words, students apply their learning to the given context or topic to create some sort of product; oftentimes, in English class, it may be an essay or piece of writing.

McTigue (2015) notes that performance tasks are more common and natural to disciplines such as the visual and performing arts or vocational-technical areas, where the creation or performance is the focus of the instruction; however, they can be used in all subject areas and grade levels. Chun (2010) notes that performance tasks are a type of inquiry-based learning used to replace more traditional forms of teaching, such as rote learning and lecture. Literary performance tasks, such as the ones included here, allow students to demonstrate their mastery of one or more content standards.

For the performance tasks presented here, designed by my colleagues and me, we have started with the specific standard or standards and created a task that requires students to apply the standards to the specific context and reading selections included.

McTigue (2015) presents seven general characteristics of good performance tasks:

- They require application of knowledge and skills, not mere recall.
- They are open ended and do not have a single correct answer.

- They establish an authentic context for the performance.
- They provide evidence that students can transfer their learning to new situations.
- They are multifaceted and involve multiple steps.
- They often integrate two or more subjects, such as reading, research, writing, technology, and presentation skills.
- They are evaluated with established criteria and rubrics.

Similarly, Chun (2010) specifies five features of performance tasks: they involve a real-world scenario, an authentic and complex process, higher-order thinking, or an authentic performance (such as an original piece of writing or a presentation) and have transparent evaluation criteria.

It is important to note that performance tasks are generally not intended to be summative tests but rather as components of learning where students are gradually moving toward mastery of particular content standards. They often require extensive time to complete and may involve students using multiple resources.

Most of the performance tasks here require that students complete a number of reading assignments in addition to the anchor text. These performance tasks intentionally incorporate informational and nonfiction texts to supplement the literary anchor text, as is preferred by Common Core State Standards. In some cases, students are asked to do research to locate appropriate informational texts for the project. Students are thus required to synthesize information from multiple sources to complete the final project or piece of writing.

In English language arts classes, teachers have traditionally focused their instruction on a piece of literature for a specific amount of time (for example, a six-week unit on *Romeo and Juliet*), but Jessica Rosevear (2015) observes that new standards, such as the Common Core, have required us to combine informational texts with literary text. As a result, many ELA teachers are now supplementing our anchor texts and pieces of literature with nonfiction/informational texts and videos.

Rosevear (2015) suggests focusing on essential questions that will provide a lens to study multiple texts. She provides a useful example of a unit on Shakespeare's *Macbeth*, which focuses on two essential questions: "What are the dangers of excessive ambition?" and "What is lost or gained in the quest for success?" In addition to *Macbeth*, other texts are also incorporated, including a short story by Amy Tan; the story of Icarus from Greek mythology; and readings from Machiavelli, Thomas Paine, Martin Luther King Jr., Nelson Mandela, and the more recent Nobel Prize winner Malala Yousafzai (Rosevear, 2015).

Another example Rosevear (2015) presents is for teaching Bradbury's dystopian novel *Fahrenheit 451*. Other texts incorporated in the task might include the First Amendment of the U.S. Constitution; the John Meacham essay "Free to Be Happy"; and Senator Margaret Chase Smith's speech to Congress called "A Declaration of Conscience," which criticized the McCarthy-era climate that oppressed free speech.

Most of the performance tasks included here incorporate many, if not all, of McTigue's (2015) characteristics. One of them is a more thematic topic (poverty) and two are for a general literary genre (poetry), but most of them are designed for specific commonly taught works of American and world literature. Each task is tied to specific Common Core State Standards, specifically the Grade 9–10 standards. Using the tasks presented here as models, you can easily design your own performance tasks for other anchor pieces, novels, and plays that you might teach in your curriculum.

For great infographic resources for some of the literary texts included, see the website https://www.coursehero.com/infographics/. Infographics are included for *Huckleberry Finn*, *The Great Gatsby*, and *Our Town*. The infographics feature information and a review of characters, themes, and literary devices used in the pieces.

All the tasks incorporate multiple texts and readings, and they can be scored using a writing rubric of your choice, perhaps one designed by your state, district, or one of the CCSS testing consortiums. Many school districts and educational organizations have developed their own rubrics for scoring writing that are aligned to Common Core. They can easily be accessed online. Turnitin.com has also developed writing rubrics aligned to Common Core.

Follow this procedure for developing your own performance tasks:

- Start with the anchor text, and then identify the specific target standards.
- Identify several nonfiction texts that can be thematically connected to the anchor text (essays, speeches, historical documents, articles, excerpts from books, reports, videos, and multimodal pieces).
- Create the essay topics or specific performance task you want students to complete.
- Identify or create a rubric that you will use to evaluate the completed tasks.

PERFORMANCE TASKS FOR SPECIFIC TEXTS

Huckleberry Finn and Nineteenth-Century Literature Performance Task

Mark Twain's classic novel *The Adventures of Huckleberry Finn* is one of the most important pieces of American literature; in fact, many literary scholars would argue it is the most important. It was written during a time of struggle in the American South due to the effects of slavery and widespread racism, but the novel is actually set in an earlier decade when slavery was still common. In many ways, the book focuses on the hypocrisy of slavery as we observe the central character of Huckleberry Finn struggle with his conscience over his friendship with Jim, the runaway slave.

Twain wrote this novel as a sequel to and to capitalize on the success of *The Adventures of Tom Sawyer*, but it surpasses Tom Sawyer's story in its profound insight and themes of race and identity. Many believe it is a novel that all American high school students should read and be familiar with. It is also one that adolescents can easily relate to as a coming-of-age story. The character of Huck struggles with an abusive and alcoholic father, is left orphaned, learns to become independent, and deals with the moral dilemmas and questions of right and wrong that growing up presents. Students also enjoy Twain's use of humor in the novel.

Twain's novel can be challenging because of the frequent passages of dialect that are used. Since the story features Huck and Jim's journey down the Mississippi River, Twain sought to characterize the many types of people living in various regions of the country at that time by re-creating in his story the regional speech forms and patterns. Thus, the book includes several long passages of dialect that can become challenging for students to read and understand. Jim's slave dialect is one of the most frequent. You might want to read through some of the passages of dialect together with students to help them become more comfortable with it.

Another aspect that you will want to deal with in teaching this book is the controversial nature of the language used. Twain's use of the "n-word" and other language can be troublesome for many students and modern-day readers. The language has made the book controversial since its publication and led to its being banned in many schools and districts. In the classroom, you should try to deal with this issue forthrightly by having a frank discussion with students about Twain's reasons for using the word and how, as readers, we must read and interpret it as a period piece, recognizing that it is a product of the time when it was written. Tell students that, as modern-day readers, it is unfair to impose our current standards and sense of "political correctness" on a work written over 150 years ago.

You might also discuss the controversy over the way the character Jim is portrayed in the book. While some readers have felt that Twain was presenting Jim as a stereotype of the black slave, others recognize that Twain was attempting to humanize Jim and create a sympathetic figure. Jim helps to convey Twain's critique of the practice of slavery.

Since several aspects of the novel can be challenging for readers, before beginning this performance task, you will want to lead students through reading and discussion of the novel. Some teachers have chosen to have students read and focus on only key excerpts and chapters from the text.

This performance task addresses the following standards:

- Reading Literature Standard 2: Determine a theme or central idea of a text and analyze in detail its development over the course of the text, including how it emerges and is shaped and refined by specific details; provide an objective summary of the text,
- Writing Standard 1: Write arguments to support claims in an analysis of substantive topics or texts, using valid reasoning and relevant and sufficient evidence.

In addition to the novel itself, there are several other reading selections included to prepare students for the essay they will be writing. Which selections they use for evidence in their paper will depend on which topic they choose. Most of the following are well-known texts and can be easily found online:

- Charlotte Perkins Gilman's short story "The Yellow Wallpaper"
- Excerpts from *My Bondage and My Freedom*, by Frederick Douglass (use the passage where Douglass describes how he was taught to read). You might instead choose to use an excerpt from the more famous Douglass book *Narrative of the Life of Frederick Douglass*.
- Abraham Lincoln's "Gettysburg Address"
- Sojourner Truth's famous speech "Ain't I a Woman?"
- The Declaration of Sentiments of the Seneca Falls Convention
- Chief Joseph's address "I Will Fight No More Forever"
- Leonard Pitts's editorial "Don't Censor Mark Twain's N Word" (this editorial was published in the *Miami Herald*, January 9, 2011, in response to the NewSouth Books publication of a sanitized version of Twain's novel).

Follow this lesson sequence for the performance task, following reading of the complete novel (or excerpts):

1. Have students complete individual reading of all the reading selections in addition to *Huckleberry Finn*. As an alternative to individual reading and note taking, you can have students read in pairs or small groups. You can also break up the readings by having some discussion or doing short activities after reading selected pieces. Have students take Cornell Notes during their reading, and ask each student to prepare three discussion questions they can use during the Socratic Seminar.
2. Organize the class for a Socratic Seminar (or another form of group discussion) on the reading selections. Students should use their Cornell Notes

and submit their written questions to the group. You will probably need to schedule one full period for the Socratic Seminar, and make sure that every student has the chance to ask at least one question. At the end of the discussion, have students write a summary of the seminar in which they identify characteristics and elements of nineteenth-century literature as reflected in the reading selections. Follow up with a whole-class discussion to check for understanding.

3. Next, students will need to understand the performance task assignment they will be expected to complete and choose one of the essay topics provided. Explain that the essay will need to draw on textual evidence from *Huckleberry Finn* and the other reading selections and that all essays must include the following:

- Introduces a precise claim
- Develops the claim with specific evidence
- Uses transitional words and phrases to link major sections
- Establishes and maintains a formal writing style
- Provides an effective conclusion

Depending on your group of students, you may want to include mini-lessons in some of these requisite writing skills prior to having students begin work on the essays. As preface to topic 4 below, one of our colleagues at a nearby high school, Pattie Sloan, had her students write letters to the editor of our local newspaper, sharing their opinions of the novel, in relation to their class study of the novel, human trafficking, and the publication of the sanitized version of *Huckleberry Finn*. While they are not reproduced here, our students read the local newspaper's editorial and Mrs. Sloan's students' letters in addition to Pitts's editorial. You will want to remove the reference to that portion from essay topic 4 when using this performance task. Have students choose one of the following topics:

- Topic 1: Write an argument in which you agree or disagree with the following statement, offering at least four pieces of evidence from multiple texts to support your position: Women, African Americans, and Native Americans in nineteenth-century America could not really be free.
- Topic 2: What is the American Dream? Write an argument essay that uses at least four pieces of evidence to show how the literature of the nineteenth century does or does not fully embody the values inherent in the American Dream.
- Topic 3: Write an argument essay that presents your position on how Mark Twain and other nineteenth-century authors address the issue of

slavery. Be sure that you establish a clear and precise claim. Use at least four pieces of evidence that support your claim.
- Topic 4: *Huckleberry Finn* has been one of the most commonly banned and censored books in American schools. Recently, a censored and sanitized version of the novel was published that removed the use of the "n-word" and other objectionable language. Read Leonard Pitts's *Miami Herald* editorial from 2011 called "Don't Censor Mark Twain's N Word." Also, read the *Statesman Journal*'s article and letters presenting Salem students' views of the controversy. You may want to do additional research to find out more about the reasons why the novel has been commonly banned in schools. Take notes, and jot down your reactions and thoughts as you read these selections. Write an essay that argues in favor of or against censorship of the novel. Should the original novel be read and discussed by students today?

4. Have students complete a pre-writing activity for their essay, such as a brainstorming, diagram, graphic organizer, list, or free write. Consider assigning a grade for completion of the pre-writing.
5. Have students prepare an outline of their paper with the claim statement clearly written at the top. Have students turn in the outline for an additional checkpoint grade, and review the claim statements, making suggestions for revision as necessary. Preparing an outline for their essay will help students more effectively organize their evidence and incorporate transitions. You may want to present a couple of sample outlines to show students the correct outline format.
6. Present a list of common transitions that students can refer to during their writing. Remind them that they need to include transitions between ideas and sections of their paper. Here is a list of common transitions:

after	also	another
as a result	consequently	during
finally	finally	first
for example	for instance	for one thing
furthermore	however	in addition
in contrast	in summary	last
last of all	meanwhile	moreover
next	next to	on one hand
on the contrary	on the other hand	otherwise
second	specifically	therefore
third	thus	to illustrate
while	yet	

7. Have students write the first draft of their paper and spend some time revising. Present a rubric or checklist for them to use during revision. You may want to incorporate a peer response activity to allow students to read others' papers and provide suggestions.
8. Have students prepare a final, typed draft of their essay.
9. Culminating activity: Have students share their essays by reading an excerpt of their paper to the class or reading and discussing their entire essays in small groups.
10. Score the essays using a scoring guide for argument writing. We use the SBA argument-writing rubric approved by our district, which scores the papers from 1 to 4 in the areas of Purpose and Focus, Organization, Elaboration of Evidence, Language and Vocabulary, and Conventions.

This performance task for *Huckleberry Finn* and nineteenth-century literature has been one of the most successful. Students have found these topics interesting and engaging, and they have generated some excellent essays, with especially impassioned essays being written on the topic of censorship of the novel. Figure 4.1 shows two of my students' essays written for this performance task. Noah's paper addresses topic 1, and Jillian's paper addresses topic 3.

Cyrano de Bergerac Performance Task

This performance task follows class study of the famous French drama from the nineteenth century *Cyrano de Bergerac*, by Edmond Rostand. The play is based on a real person of the same name but is a fictionalized work, written in dramatic Alexandrine format. *Cyrano* has been immensely popular since it was first published and has also been adapted into movie versions, opera, and other forms. The main character is a cadet in the French army, well known as a duelist and also a creative and gifted poet and musician. However, he is afflicted with self-doubt due to his extremely large nose, which prevents him from confessing his love to the beautiful heiress Roxanne. Although the play comes out of the era of classical French drama, it does not fit into any of the literary movements of the time.

This performance task asks students to read several informational texts in addition to the play itself and culminates in the writing of a definition essay, a type of informative/explanatory writing. This task was designed by my colleague Cara Fortey, who uses the play *Cyrano de Bergerac* in her world literature and philosophy classes.

The purpose of a definition essay is to explain for readers the definition of a term or concept, which in many cases may also involve persuading the

Noah's paper:

With Liberty and Justice for All (White Men)

As the decades pass by, many of us allow ourselves to think that the problem of discrimination and prejudice has lessened and we may pat ourselves on the back. However, it can be helpful to look back at how societies used to function, so we can learn from them and help fix the shortcomings in the present day. Limitations of certain people's freedoms in the past and even in the present are often imposed by public attitudes of gender and racial bias. For example, in America during the 1800s, several groups of people were victims of prejudice. Evidence of racist and sexist public sentiment can often be found in literature written during this time period and can help demonstrate how women, Native Americans, and African Americans could not really be free in nineteenth century America.

Native Americans were one group that was discriminated against a great deal in the 1800s in America. By the nineteenth century, many Native American populations were living on reservations, which were segregated by their very nature. Chief Joseph of the Nez Perce, Native American Chief, and his speech "I Will Fight No More Forever," demonstrates the anguish and misery felt by Native Americans as a result of oppression in a white American society. Joseph remarks, "I am tired; my heart is sick and sad," indicating how much conflict with other Americans had damaged his community and way of life. While Native Americans were not commonly enslaved in the 1800s, they still would not officially win some of the civil rights they had been fighting for until the Indian Civil Rights Act of 1968.

In addition to Native Americans, African Americans were among the groups that suffered from discrimination in the 1800s. Although an increasing number of people were opposed to slavery, the idea was still widely accepted. Mark Twain's novel, *Huckleberry Finn*, accurately reflects the prejudice many Americans held against African Americans in nineteenth century America. Huckleberry Finn, the main character in Twain's novel, has been raised, surrounded and influenced mostly by slave-owning adults. This influence is evident in Chapter 15 after Huck plays a trick on Jim, his formerly enslaved companion. After seeing that he has hurt Jim's feelings, Huck comments, "It was fifteen minutes before I could work myself up to go humble myself to a nigger; but I done it, and I warn't ever sorry for it afterwards, neither." Even though Huck does apologize, he was still challenged to do so because of the racist attitudes of the time that influenced him and that were held by most white adults.

Another example of African American racism from *Huckleberry Finn* is in Chapter 26, when the duke, a white con man, comments on what he thinks is the natural behavior of slaves. The duke is referring to a hypothetical situation in which an African American slave may have run across some stolen money, referring to it as "duds." He says, ". . . you know the nigger that does up the rooms will get an order to box these duds up and put 'em away; and do you reckon a nigger can run across money and not borrow some of it?" This statement has a tone that implies that all or most African Americans are thieves—which is ironic, since the duke is a con man. Now, the duke's opinion is probably on the more extreme side of the spectrum in terms of racism—at least in the Northern United States. However, many white Americans at the time, and even some African Americans, accepted some form of these racist attitudes.

Figure 4.1. Sample Student Essays
Source: Student work reprinted with permission.

While there were many racist attitudes that limited the freedoms of African and Native Americans, there was also a great deal of sexual discrimination in nineteenth century America that limited the freedoms of women of all races. "The Declaration of Sentiments," issued in Seneca Falls in 1848, recognizes the view that, "The history of mankind is a history of repeated injuries and usurpations on the part of man toward woman. . ." The Nineteenth Amendment, granting women the right to vote in America, would not be added to the United States Constitution until 1920. Not only that, but a great deal of social pressures and expectations around "traditional gender roles" in child care and housekeeping limited women's ability to choose an alternate path if she so desired.

While the image of nineteenth century America may be of national progress, it wasn't always perfect for everyone. Westward expansion and industrialization often came at the cost of the people already there, like Native Americans, many of whom were forced to live on reservations by white settlers. As the rapidly progressing machines in the Northern United States quickly increased the nation's producing power and capacity, the Southern U.S. attempted to ramp up production as well to supply the raw materials required to take full advantage of this industrial advancement. This often resulted in more slavery or slave owners treating their slaves worse in attempt to gain more labor. Women's average position in American society was not particularly worse than in times prior thanks to societal pressures, but it was still not close to being up to our current ideas of freedom and equality. Looking back on some of the social and economic restraints imposed on women, African Americans, and Native Americans in the United States during the 1800's, it is apparent that these people lived with greatly restricted freedoms.

Jillian's paper:

Slavery Stance

During the nineteenth century, slavery was a common source of inspiration for literature. Although each author approached the topic in a slightly different manner, famous works including "The Gettysburg Address," *My Bondage and My Freedom*, and *Huckleberry Finn*, unanimously refused to misrepresent the effect of slavery on society. Nineteenth century authors boldly embraced the subject of slavery through their revelations, recollections, language, and conflicts. Despite past and present criticism on the way slavery was confronted in literature, the statement made by each work, set a precedent for acknowledging the equality of all men.

Speeches during the nineteenth century addressed slavery in a thoughtful manner that influenced literate and illiterate people alike. The carefully-calculated "Gettysburg Address," written and presented by Abraham Lincoln, cleverly discussed the failure to enforce the proposition that America was built upon. With the speech, President Lincoln reminds listeners that originally, America was "conceived in liberty, and dedicated to the proposition that all men are created equal." Afterward, however, President Lincoln draws a sharp contrast between the past promises by identifying the losses recently experienced in the Civil War. In this manner, the Gettysburg Address boldly embraces slavery by acknowledging that it was not a founding principle of America. Consequently, the terse speech given by President Lincoln manages to reveal the absurd nature of fighting over something we know is wrong. By refusing to deny the effects of slavery, the Gettysburg Address effectively addresses the topic by leaving the crowd with a fresh perspective regarding slavery.

Figure 4.1. *(continued)*

The inside perspective of slavery provided by the *My Bondage and My Freedom*, by Frederick Douglass, is another example of a nineteenth century writer refusing to misrepresent the effects of slavery. As an escaped slave, Frederick Douglass recalls, in his autobiography, the oppression he experienced that nearly prevented him from reaching his true potential as a writer. Within the narrative, Douglass depicts the attempts made to keep him, the slave, illiterate and dependent on his masters to meet society's expectations. Originally, Douglass was taught how to read and write until the master requested that his education be stopped: "My mistress—who had begun to teach me—was suddenly checked in her benevolent design, by the strong advice of her husband." In publicizing his experience, Frederick Douglass removes America's blinders by embracing his past and depicting the harm inflicted by denying a person the right to be educated and free.

Ultimately, Douglass concludes that slavery had come between him and his potential. Furthermore, the issue of slavery had cursed his relationship with the mistress from the beginning: "Nature had made us friends: slavery made us enemies. . . She aimed to keep me ignorant and I resolved to know." Later on, Douglass makes a pivotal revelation regarding his perspective of his suppression: "It was slavery—not its mere incidents—that I hated. I had been cheated. I saw through the attempt to keep me in ignorance." Above all, however, by calling slavery out by name, Frederick Douglass played a crucial role in revealing the need to deny its presence any longer: "The feeding and clothing me well, could not atone for taking my liberty from me." Essentially, by publishing his story, Frederick Douglass takes an affirmative stance against accepting the existence of slavery.

In addition to Frederick Douglass, Mark Twain confronts the existence of slavery through the language used in his novel *Huckleberry Finn*. Granted, Mark Twain has received a lot of criticism regarding his decision to use the uncensored N-word; by using the word he preserves the integrity of the story. Specifically, young Huck consistently refers to Jim as such and makes additional comments regarding the obvious difference between the slave and himself as supported by society: "I made Jim lay down in the canoe and cover up with the quilt, because if he set up people could tell he was a nigger a good ways off." Furthermore, the contrast between Huck and Jim's manner of speech, in itself, acknowledges the relentless effects of slavery on a person's confidence, education, and freedom. The ironic and wishful statements made by Jim, force the reader to question everything they were raised to believe about slavery. For instance, Mark Twain has Jim innocently question his unfair treatment he receives in his understandable desire to be free: "Yes: en I's rich now, come to look at it. I owns myself, en "is wuth eight hund'd dollars. I wisht I had de money, I wouldn't want no mo'." The novel *Huckleberry Finn* uses irony to make a controversial statement regarding the issue of slavery.

Alongside irony and language, Mark Twain expertly weaves thoughtful conflicts throughout *Huckleberry Finn* in order to question the reader's mindset toward slavery. Although the King and Duke are not, in fact, who they claim to be, they make crucial statements regarding the unfortunate case of slaves that just as easily could have been on the other end of the spectrum: "It ain't my fault you warn't born a duke, it ain't your fault you warn't born a king—so what's the use to worry." Later on, when the con men are finally captured, Mark Twain takes the opportunity to make a thoughtful revelation concerning the way humans treat each other: "It was a dreadful thing to see. Human beings *can* be awful cruel to one another." When all was said and done, Jim provided the most valuable

Figure 4.1. *(continued)*

perspective regarding the influence of slavery: "Jim he couldn't see no sense in the most of it, but he allowed we was white folks and knowed better than him, so he was satisfied."

Literature provided a platform for the discussion of slavery during the nineteenth century by providing a safe area of discussion where ideas could be represented symbolically, rather than directly. As a result, nineteenth century writers expressed a similar desire to confront the issue of slavery through revelations, recollections, language, and conflicts. Works such as the "Gettysburg Address," *My Bondage and My Freedom*, and *Huckleberry Finn* bravely addressed slavery by questioning the very existence of its practices and its morality. The published stances made against slavery were pivotal in representing once socially-acceptable practices in a new light that revealed a fresh perspective.

Figure 4.1. *(continued)*

reader that one's particular definition is a valid one. Such essays are often developed with specific examples. In some contexts, they are called "expanded definitions" because a number of techniques are used to expand or develop the definition of a term that is generally abstract or conceptual.

You might have students practice with this form by asking them to write short essays or quick writes to define terms such as slob, con artist, good neighbor, pessimist, scapegoat, hypocrisy, jealousy, bravery, persistence, laziness, curiosity, responsibility, obsession, terrorism, idealism, spirituality, heroism, and procrastination.

Since *Cyrano de Bergerac* is a play, conduct a class reading of the play rather than assigning it as independent reading. Assign or have students alternate reading parts, assigning each part to one student and reading aloud to give a more realistic, dramatic sense of the work for students.

CCSS Standards addressed in this performance task follow:

- Reading Literature Standard 2: Determine a theme or central idea of a text, and analyze in detail its development over the course of the text, including how it emerges and is shaped and refined by specific details; provide an objective summary of the text.
- Writing Standard 2: Write informative/explanatory texts to examine and convey complex ideas, concepts, and information clearly and accurately through the effective selection, organization, and analysis of content.

Follow this lesson sequence for the performance task after reading of the complete play:

1. Provide students time to read, annotate, and discuss the following supplementary readings, taking notes as they read. All of these reading selections focus on the concept of beauty. They represent cultural, scientific, and philosophical approaches to defining "beauty." Students' own definition papers will be modeled on the readings related to the concept of beauty. If

students choose to define another concept, you have the option of requiring them to conduct research to find additional source material related to that concept, which can be used as support:

Cultural approaches to beauty:

- "Geography of Beauty: Beauty Is in the Eyes of the Beholder, Based on Geography," http://geography.about.com/od/culturalgeography/a/Geography-Of-Beauty.htm
- "Beauty: Culture-Specific or Universally Defined?" by Gad Saad, http://www.psychologytoday.com/blog/homo-consumericus/201004/beauty-culture-specific-or-universally-defined
- "Around the World, Notions of Beauty Can Be a Real Beast," by Maureen Pao, http://www.npr.org/sections/parallels/2013/09/26/226565319/around-the-world-notions-of-beauty-can-be-a-real-beast

Scientific approaches to beauty:

- "The Math Behind Beauty: A Plastic Surgeon Computes the Perfect Face," by Bruno Maddox, http://discovermagazine.com/2007/jun/blinded-by-science
- "The Enigma of Beauty," by Cathy Newman, http://science.nationalgeographic.com/science/health-and-human-body/human-body/enigma-beauty/
- "The Science of Beauty," by Xenocrates, http://xenlogic.wordpress.com/2009/02/04/the-science-of-beauty/

Philosophical approaches to beauty:

- Stanford Encyclopedia of Philosophy definition of "Beauty" (2016), http://plato.stanford.edu/entries/beauty/
- "How Do Philosophers Think About Beauty? How Do We Know, Appreciate, and Value Beauty?" by Andrea Borghini (2016), https://www.thoughtco.com/how-do-philosophers-think-about-beauty-2670642
- Philosophy of Beauty online lecture/text by University of Minnesota, Duluth, instructor John H. Brown, http://faculty.philosophy.umd.edu/jhbrown/beautyintro/

2. Introduce students to the concept of the definition essay as one that defines a term or concept in depth by providing personal commentary and examples of what the specific term means. The play itself deals with various concepts, such as honor, bravery, and beauty, and the writing task allows

students to develop their own expanded definition of the concept and support it with evidence from the play and other readings. Students will be writing a personal, extended definition of an abstract term by linking or comparing the term to a previous definition and illustrating how that term should be applied. Students will also be expected to link their definition and chosen topic to *Cyrano de Bergerac*. Clarify that they will be expected to bolster their definition by quoting lines and scenes from the play.
3. Present the following as possible topics for definition, ones that can also be related to themes and ideas from the play: beauty, honesty, bravery, love, happiness, confidence, integrity, and romance.
4. Next, present students with a possible outline or structure for organizing the paper, such as the following. Clarify that there are other possible structures and ways of organizing and that students do not have to slavishly follow this outline:

   I. Introduction
      A. Attention-getter
         1. The traditional or dictionary definition that may provide a basis for your personal definition
         2 A contradictory image that may help illustrate the definition
      B. Thesis: State your definition of the term. If you can write the definition by stating specific subpoints, it will be easier to structure the writing of the rest of the paper.
   II. Body
      A. Point 1
         1. The first part of your definition
         2. An example to illustrate the point
         3. Analysis of how the example illustrates the point
      B. Point 2
         1. The second part of your definition
         2. Example to illustrate the point
         3. Analysis of how the example illustrates the point
      C. Point 3
         1. The third part of your definition
         2. Example to illustrate the point
         3. Analysis of how the example illustrates the point
   III. Conclusion
      A. Review of your definition's main points
      B. Closing and summary
         1. Sometimes, a reference back to the opening attention-getter is a good way to unify the essay.
         2. You may want to close with an explanation of how your definition has affected you.

5. Unless you are working with advanced students, it would be best to lead students through the writing process: pre-writing, drafting, revising, final draft, editing, and proofreading. Provide a list of transitions, such as the one presented in the previous section, and provide specific strategies for revision.
6. Final reminders to present to students:

- Check to be sure you have a specific thesis that explains how the term is defined.
- Follow your outline and remember to include specific examples and discussion of the examples. Modify the outline if needed.
- Use specific examples to illustrate each point—examples help readers to visualize how the definition can be applied.
- Provide good transitions to link all the parts of the essay.
- Have a strong conclusion that brings the parts of the definition together and leaves readers with an image of how the definition is applied.
- Proofread carefully.

7. Have students share their final definition essays in small groups or with a gallery walk.
8. Score these papers with a rubric designed for informative/explanatory/expository writing.

The Great Gatsby Performance Task

The Great Gatsby, by F. Scott Fitzgerald, is a classic novel and one of the most important American works of the twentieth century. It is a period piece, written during and set in the 1920s. The novel compellingly captures all the excitement and glitter of the period known as the Roaring Twenties, a fascinating historical period. In some ways, the 1920s was a raucous interlude between world wars, a time of economic boom and expanding wealth, the era of prohibition and the resulting underground bootleg industry, and also a time of conformity and intolerance. The era marked the development and expansion of new technologies: the automobile, the motion picture, and radio. It was also known as "The Jazz Age," when New Orleans–style jazz became vastly popular, as did a variety of new leisure activities, such as baseball and golf.

The author of this tragic story of the search for love, F. Scott Fitzgerald, was himself a product of the 1920s and was perhaps obsessed with themes of love and success. He was known to be something of a playboy, and he and his wife, Zelda, were well-known celebrities of the time. They lived as expatriates in Paris for several years, establishing friendships with other American writers, such as Hemingway. While he published several novels, *The Great*

Gatsby is considered Fitzgerald's greatest work. We have found students are absolutely fascinated with this book, its characters and setting and the exasperating love triangle the story presents.

This performance task addresses the following CCSS Standards:

- Reading Literature Standard 1: Cite strong and thorough textual evidence to support analysis of what the text says explicitly as well as inferences drawn from the text.
- Reading Literature Standard 2: Determine a theme or central idea of a text and analyze in detail its development over the course of the text, including how it emerges and is shaped and refined by specific details; provide an objective summary of the text.
- Writing Standard 1: Write arguments to support claims in an analysis of substantive topics or texts, using valid reasoning and relevant and sufficient evidence.

In addition to reading of the complete novel itself, there are several other reading selections included that students should draw from for the essay they will be writing:

- President Barack Obama's Inaugural Address, January 21, 2013. (You can use either a print transcript of the speech or a video recording. *New York Times*, *Wall Street Journal*, and C-Span versions are all available on youtube.com: https://www.youtube.com/watch?v=zncqb-n3zMo.) In this address, Obama speaks of his vision of America and the American Dream.
- Greta Olson, "Reconsidering Unreliability: Fallible and Trustworthy Narrators," *Narrative*, Volume 11, Issue 1, January 2003, page 93+. This source is a lengthy, scholarly article, so you may want to use only excerpts from it. It can be found by doing a database search.
- Samuel Chase Coale, "Fitzgerald, F. Scott," World Book Student. *World Book*, 2016
- "Roaring Twenties," World Book Student. *World Book*, 2016
- Video: Defining the American Dream: *New York Times*, May 7, 2009, https://www.nytimes.com/video/us/1194840031120/defining-the-american-dream.htmlhttps://www.nyt
- Anna Wulick, "Is Gatsby Great? Analyzing the Title of *The Great Gatsby*." SAT/ACT Prep Online Guides and Tips. PrepScholar. April 29, 2016, blog.prepscholar.com/is-gatsby-great-explaining-the-title
- Kate O'Connor, "Lost Generation," Great Writers Inspire Series. University of Oxford, http://writersinspire.org/content/lost-generation
- Student paper by Alyzaanne: "Nick Carraway: An Unreliable Narrator," posted October 19, 2013, http://alyzaanne.wordpress.com/2013/10/19/

nick-carraway-an-unreliable-narrator/. There are several other online articles about Nick Caraway and his reliability as a narrator that you can choose from. You may also want to include a definition of the term "unreliable narrator" from a handbook of literary terms.
- You might also consider including James Baldwin's essay "The American Dream and the American Negro," originally published in the *New York Times*, March 7, 1965, http://www.nytimes.com/books/98/03/29/specials/baldwin-dream.html. This article provides more historical context of the concept of the American Dream from a minority perspective.

Follow this lesson sequence for the performance task, following reading of the complete novel:

1. Have students complete individual reading of the nonfiction selections in addition to *The Great Gatsby*. You may want to break up the readings by having some discussion or doing short activities after reading the selected pieces. Have students take Cornell Notes during their reading, which they can use as a source of evidence when they write their essays.
2. As an alternative activity prior to writing the essays, you may want to organize a Socratic Seminar or some other form of group discussion on the reading selections, similar to the procedure used for the previous *Huckleberry Finn* performance task.
3. Next, have students choose one of the following essay topics. The argument prompts for this task were developed by Matthew Isom. Explain that they will need to have "relevant and sufficient evidence" from the novel and other readings to support their essay's claim. The essay should include the following:

   - A precise claim
   - Specific evidence
   - Transitional words and phrases to link major sections
   - A formal writing style
   - An effective conclusion

Depending on the particular group of students you are working with, you may want to include some mini-lessons for these elements to help students prepare for writing their essays. Present the following essay topics.

- Topic 1: Is Fitzgerald's novel a story of love that embraces American ideals or a satirical commentary on the American Dream? Use specific evidence from the text and quotations to support your thesis.
- Topic 2: In chapter 6, when Nick says, "You can't repeat the past," Gatsby replies, "Can't repeat the past? Why, of course you can!" Gatsby

then recalls a time from the past when he had kissed Daisy. Does Gatsby misuse the past and his memories in order to survive in the present? Does he exemplify the characteristics of the "Lost Generation"?
- Topic 3: Fitzgerald considered several possible titles for his novel. It was originally titled *On the Road to West Egg*, then *Trimalchio*, then *Under the Red White and Blue*, and then *Gold-Hatted Gatsby*, before he decided on *The Great Gatsby*. Write an essay that argues that *The Great Gatsby* is an appropriate title for the book or that proposes a new title and explains the reasons for the choice.
- Topic 4: At the end of chapter 3, Nick says, "I am one of the few honest people that I have ever known." Do you believe he is truly honest? Are his descriptions and interpretations of the characters and events reliable or biased? Is he a reliable or unreliable narrator, and how do you know?
- Topic 5: Study the last page of the novel. The famous concluding line is, "Gatsby believed in the green light, the orgiastic future that year by year recedes before us. It eluded us then, but that's no matter—tomorrow we will run faster, stretch out our arms farther. . . . And one fine morning—". Explain why Fitzgerald left the last sentence unfinished? What is the "one fine morning" referring to? Do humans always live on our hopes and dreams for the future? How does the novel explore this theme?

4. Have students complete a pre-writing activity for their essay, such as a brainstorming, diagram, graphic organizer, list, or free write. Consider assigning a grade for completion of the pre-write.
5. Have students prepare an outline for their paper, with the claim statement clearly written at the top. Have students turn in the outline to you for a checkpoint grade, and review the claim statement, making suggestions for revision as necessary. Preparing an outline for their essay will help students more effectively organize their evidence and incorporate transitions.
6. Present a list of common transitions that students can refer to during their writing. Remind them that they need to include transitions between ideas and sections of their paper.
7. Have students write the first draft of their paper, and then spend some time revising. Present a rubric or checklist for them to use during revision. You may want to incorporate a peer response activity to allow students to read others' papers and provide suggestions.
8. Have students prepare a final, typed draft of their essay.
9. As a culminating activity, have students share their essays by reading a portion of the paper to the class or reading and discussing the essay in small groups.

10. Score the essays using a scoring guide for argument writing. We use the SBA argument-writing rubric approved by our district, which scores the paper from 1 to 4 in the areas of Purpose and Focus, Organization, Elaboration of Evidence, Language and Vocabulary, and Conventions.

Our Town Performance Task

Thornton Wilder's classic play *Our Town* is a Pulitzer Prize–winning drama, written in 1938. Many find the play to be a profoundly beautiful drama, and modern-day students respond to its simplicity, beauty, and powerful truths as well. The play appears to be a simple story of small-town life in the early twentieth century, set in Grover's Corners, New Hampshire. In reality, it portrays powerful truths about the human condition and all the beauty and wonder of life that most humans fail to notice or appreciate. It is a reminder to all of us that we should appreciate all the beauty of life before it's gone.

In the last act of the play, the Stage Manager states, "There's something way down deep that's eternal about every human being." This powerful theme is combined with the heroine Emily's observation, after her life has ended tragically, that "live people don't understand." The playwright masterfully used the simple setting and ordinary characters to convey powerful truths about human beings and our fragility. Jeremy McCarter (2009), in a *Newsweek* review, called the play "a harrowing story about human limitation—all the beauty and value we fail to recognize in our day-to-day lives."

Our Town is also an interesting piece from a theatrical perspective. It is known for its simple setting and lack of props and scenery, an intentional move by the dramatist to allow the audience to focus on the characters, universal representations of ordinary human beings everywhere. Young students today can relate to the stories of the young people in this play, who like all of us, experience young love, sometimes have problematic relationships with family members, and suffer tragic losses as well.

This performance task addresses the following CCSS:

- Reading Literature Standard 1: Cite strong and thorough textual evidence to support analysis of what the text says explicitly as well as inferences drawn from the text.
- Reading Literature Standard 2: Determine a theme or central idea of a text and analyze in detail its development over the course of the text, including how it emerges and is shaped and refined by specific details; provide an objective summary of the text.

- Writing Standard 1: Write arguments to support claims in an analysis of substantive topics or texts, using valid reasoning and relevant and sufficient evidence.

In addition to the play itself, there are several other reading selections that students read to prepare for the essay they will be writing. Which selections they refer to for evidence will depend on which essay topic they choose. You might want to intersperse reading of the other sources with reading of the play. These selections can easily be located online and through library databases:

- Edward Collimore, "Thornton Wilder's 'Our Town' Has Roots in Moorestown," *Philadelphia Enquirer*, October 1, 2012
- Jeremy McCarter "Something Wilder," *Newsweek*, September 28, 2009
- Walter Ault, "Irony and Timelessness of 'Our Town' Not Lost on Our Time," *Montgomery Media*, Tuesday, January 8, 2013, http://www.montgomerynews.com/entertainment/irony-and-timelessness-of-our-town-not-lost-on-our/article_a8319ad9-a32c-5bb0-987e-b739042772e3.html
- An excerpt of Critical Analysis on Our Town from the Thornton Wilder Society, http://www.twildersociety.org/works/our-town/
- An excerpt from a handbook of literary terms: Literary definition of "Tragedy" and "Tragic Hero." This excerpt can be taken from any handbook of literary terms, preferably a definition that refers to Aristotle's original explanation of classical tragedy.
- Arthur Ballet, "Our Town as Classical Tragedy," in *Readings on Our Town*, edited by Thomas Siebold, San Diego, Greenhaven Press, 2000, pp. 74–82. This is a well-known piece of literary criticism of the play. You can use a brief summary of Ballet's article rather than the entire text.
- George D. Stephens, "Our Town as Failed Tragedy," in *Readings on Our Town*, edited by Thomas Siebold, San Diego, Greenhaven Press, 2000, pp. 83–93. This is also a well-known piece of literary criticism and a challenge to Ballet's interpretation of the play. You might use a brief summary of this article rather than the complete text.
- George D. Stephens, "Our Town—Great American Tragedy?" *Modern Drama*, Vol. 1, No. 4, February 1959, pp. 258–64.

There are numerous other articles, reviews, and published discussions of Wilder's play that you could use to supplement or replace some of the sources here. The critical debate about whether *Our Town* is a tragedy is necessary, however, for students who choose essay topic 4.

Follow this lesson sequence for the performance task:

1. Assign members of the class to read particular roles. Complete a class reading of the play aloud. You may also want to choose a few key scenes and have students prepare to act them out. There are about twenty speaking roles in the play, and many of them very small, so most of the class can have a speaking part. You will want to make sure a strong reader is assigned to the central role of the Stage Manager. Pause between each of the three acts of the play and have students do some review, discussion, and activities to guide their reading and understanding of the play.
2. Assign students to read the supplementary texts as well, either independently or in pairs or small groups. Have them take Cornell Notes during their reading of the supplementary texts.
3. Schedule a whole-group discussion or Socratic Seminar to engage in discussion of the play and the other readings.
4. You may also want to schedule class viewing of one of the film or stage versions of *Our Town*. There is an old movie version from the 1930s and a great 1970s film version, with Hal Holbrook and Robby Benson.
5. Next, present the essay topic options to students. Explain to students that they will be writing an argument essay about the play *Our Town* and that they will be expected to draw evidence from the supplementary readings provided as well as from the play itself. Student essays will need to include a precise claim, specific evidence, transitional words and phrases, a formal writing style, and an effective conclusion. The following are the five essay topics:

    - Topic 1: Some have said that *Our Town* is a simple play, a nostalgic reflection on small-town life in the early 1900s. Others argue that it has a much deeper and more profound meaning. McCarter describes it as a "harrowing story about human limitation—all the beauty and value we fail to recognize in our everyday lives." Write your own argument about the meaning and significance of the play and its themes, using specific evidence for support.
    - Topic 2: In *Our Town*, the Stage Manager states the following famous line: "We all know that something is eternal . . . and that something has to do with human beings. . . . There's something way down deep that's eternal about every human being." Also, throughout the play, there are frequent references to the stars, moon, and universe. Think carefully about these elements, and make an argument about the theme that Wilder was trying to convey. Be sure to support your argument with specific evidence from the play and other sources.
    - Topic 3: It has been said that *Our Town* is no longer relevant to audiences today. While some viewers have found it boring and unaffecting,

other readers and viewers are profoundly moved by it. Use direct references to the play and evidence from other sources to support an argument about whether the play is relevant to modern readers.
- Topic 4: Some critics have argued that *Our Town* is a modern tragedy in the classical literary sense. Review the definition of tragedy and the brief pieces of criticism provided, and then write your own argument about whether *Our Town* is a tragedy. Use evidence from the play and other sources to support your argument.
- Topic 5: *Our Town* is famous for its use of minimalist staging techniques: plain, bare stage and lack of props and scenery. Write an essay that makes an argument about the effects of Wilder's staging techniques on the audience. Include in your argument evidence of how well the use of the stark, simple setting and lack of theatrical devices reinforce the play's themes.

6. Have students complete a pre-writing activity for their essay, such as a brainstorming, diagram, graphic organizer, list, or free write. Assign a grade for completion of the pre-write.
7. Have students prepare an outline for their paper with their claim statement clearly written at the top. Have students turn in the outline for an additional checkpoint grade. Review the claim statements, making suggestions for revision as necessary. Preparing an outline for the essay will help students more effectively organize their evidence and incorporate transitions. You may want to present a couple of sample outlines to show students correct outline format.
8. Present a list of common transitions that students can refer to during their writing. Remind them that they need to include transitions between ideas and sections of their paper.
9. Have students write the first draft of their paper and spend some time revising. Present a rubric or checklist for them to use during revision. You may also want to incorporate a peer response activity to allow students to read others' papers and provide suggestions.
10. Have students prepare a final, typed draft of their essay.
11. As a culminating activity, have students share their essays by reading an excerpt of their paper to the class or reading and discussing their entire essays in small groups. A fun, additional culminating activity is to have students work independently, in pairs, or in small groups to prepare a dramatic reading of a monologue, passage of dialogue, or scene from the play. Some students may choose to perform an excerpt from one of the Stage Manager's monologues, reenact the scene between George and Emily at their windows at the end of Act One, the famous scene with

George and Emily in Mr. Morgan's drugstore in Act Two, or Emily's famous "Goodbye, world" monologue from Act Three.
12. Score the essays, using a scoring guide for argument writing. We use the SBA argument-writing rubric approved by our district, which scores the papers from 1 to 4 in the areas of Purpose and Focus, Organization, Elaboration of Evidence, Language and Vocabulary, and Conventions.

Of Mice and Men Performance Task

John Steinbeck's classic novella *Of Mice and Men* is a short yet powerful story. Set during the Great Depression, it tells the story of two itinerant farmworkers traveling from one job to the next, all the while dreaming of owning a piece of land and a place of their own where they can "live off the fat of the land." The novel can actually be described as a parable about friendship and human dignity. The novel focuses on themes of compassion, dignity, the American Dream, and loneliness.

The unforgettable ending of the novel has an intense impact on readers, as one of the main characters, George, must make the ultimate sacrifice. The other main character, Lennie, is mentally handicapped, a gentle giant, and a true friend to George. The novel reveals Steinbeck's classic literary style, is very accessible for high school students, and contains rich themes that can spark great discussion and writing among students. This performance task was designed by my colleague Sandy Graham.

This performance task addresses the following standards:

- Reading Literature Standard 1: Cite strong and thorough textual evidence to support analysis of what the text says explicitly as well as inferences drawn from the text.
- Reading Literature Standard 2: Determine a theme or central idea of a text and analyze in detail its development over the course of the text, including how it emerges and is shaped and refined by specific detail.
- Writing Standard 1: Write arguments to support claims in an analysis of substantive topics or texts, using valid reasoning and relevant and sufficient evidence.

In addition to the novel itself, there are several other reading and video selections included that you should use to help students prepare for the essay they will be writing:

- After reading of the novel, have students watch the 1992 movie version, directed by Gary Sinise and starring Gary Sinise and John Malkovich. You

could also use shorter YouTube clips from the film as an alternative to the entire film. Have students draw comparisons between the novel and film versions.
- An essay by John Steinbeck called "America and Americans: Is the American Dream Even Possible?" http://www.mychandlerschools.org/cms/lib6/AZ01001175/Centricity/Domain/7121/AmericaNAmericans_article_steinbeck.pdf
- A PowerPoint presentation called "Loneliness and Isolation in *Of Mice and Men*." http://www.worldofteaching.com/englishliteraturepowerpoints.html
- "On the Road to Tragedy: Mice, Candy, and Land in Of Mice and Men," by Bert Cardullo, *American Drama*, Vol. 16, No. 1, 2007. Available from General One File, Gale Databases.
- "Of Mice and Men," by Angela D. Hickey. *Masterplots*, Fourth Edition, 2010, pp. 1–3. Available from EbscoHost databases.
- Script of the play version of *Of Mice and Men*, from *Read* magazine, Vol. 56, No. 1, August 25, 2006, pp. 4–13. Available from EbscoHost Literary Reference Center. You may want to conduct a class reading of the play version as an additional activity.
- "Of Mice and Men" by Peter Lesca, from *The Wide World of John Steinbeck*, 1958. Reprinted in *The American Dream*, from Bloom's Literary Themes Series, edited by Harold Bloom, 2009, pp. 133–140.
- Jonathan Leaf, "Of Mice and Melodrama," *New Criterion*, Vol. 26, No. 4, pp. 84–87. Available from EbscoHost Literary Reference Center.

Follow this lesson sequence for the performance task after reading of the complete novel:

1. In addition to individual reading of the complete novel, have students read and watch all of the supplementary texts included. Supplementary readings can be interspersed with reading of the novel if you prefer, and you may want to engage students in some discussion and activities based on the readings as well. Have students take Cornell Notes during their reading.
2. Tell students they will be writing an essay that will attempt to persuade the audience to agree with their position on a controversial subject related to the novel. Their audience will be adolescents or adult readers of the novel. They should assume that the audience knows the book's plot and characters, so it is not necessary to include a plot summary in the essay. Students should use a formal, academic writing style and tone.
3. Have students choose one of the following questions as the starting point for their essay:

- Should a mentally handicapped person be held responsible for his or her actions?
- According to your own definition of "friendship," did George and Lennie have a true friendship?
- How does the novel depict the American Dream?
- How are many of the characters affected by loneliness?
- Is Curley's wife responsible for her own death?
- When, if ever, is violence an appropriate and necessary action? Should violence be used to solve a conflict?
- Should George have killed Lennie?

Students may have other ideas or come up with additional controversial questions related to the novel, so leave open the possibility for them to generate their own essay question.

4. Specify for students the specific organizational requirements for the essay:

- An introduction that provides context and includes a thesis statement
- At least three supporting paragraphs
- Details and quotes from the novel and other reading selections in each supporting paragraph
- Effective transitions
- Support arranged emphatically from weakest to strongest
- A conclusion that restates the thesis and provides a satisfying ending

5. Clarify for students that you will score their essays using the SBA writing rubric (or some other rubric for argument essays). You may want to review the specific descriptors on the rubric with students ahead of time.

6. Provide students with an essay planning sheet, such as the one in figure 4.2. Students should complete the planning sheet to organize their essays before they start writing. Work with students on the writing of the introduction. Tell them that paragraph one should start with an attention-grabber, such as a rhetorical question, a quotation, a flashback, a shocking generalization, or something interesting that will attract the reader's attention. Next, instruct students to include in the introduction the author's full name (John Steinbeck), the title of the novel italicized, and a brief plot summary that provides context for your argument. Finally, end the introduction paragraph with the thesis statement: the writer's position on the topic, the argument. Provide students with the graphic organizer in figure 4.3, which includes an example of an introductory paragraph.

Essay Planning Sheet

What is my thesis statement? (Write it in the form of an answer to the question you started out with):

Why do I believe this to be true?

    A.

    B.

    C.

    D.

What examples from the book and other sources could I use to help support my opinion? (Write specific quotes from the novel and page numbers, if possible)

    A.

    B.

    C.

    D.

    E.

    F.

Essay organization and outline:

My introduction with an attention getter:

_____

_____

_____

My first piece of support (the weakest of my three major points):

_____

_____

_____

Figure 4.2. Planning Sheet

My second piece of support (the second best of my three major points)
My third piece of support (the strongest of my three major points)

Figure 4.2. *(continued)*

If necessary, provide similar specific instructions to help students structure and organize their body paragraphs. Students often struggle with writing an effective conclusion, so you may want to use a similar graphic organizer or a sample conclusion paragraph, such as the following:

While the moral dilemma faced by George at the end of *Of Mice and Men* is problematic at best, a close examination of his actions and motivations reveal that he was justified in his decision to kill his best friend. Although Lennie probably was not responsible for his actions, his inability to learn and remember coupled with his great physical strength made him an ever-present threat to others and a liability to George. Furthermore, _____ _____. Finally, _____ _____. In the final analysis, the moral quagmire that Steinbeck presents us with serves as a poignant reminder that each of us may someday hold another's life in our hands. And should that day come, the question would be the same as the one answered so decisively by George: Can I do the right thing?

7. While students are working on their essays, provide them with a list of transitions, and remind them that they need to include transition words and phrases between ideas and paragraphs.
8. Incorporate a peer response activity to allow students to read others' papers, and provide some suggestions. Use a checklist or peer review form.
9. Have students prepare a final, typed copy of their essays and share their essays with the class by reading an excerpt of the paper.

Graphic Organizer for the Introductory Paragraph

Attention Getter:

Plot summary with mention of book title and author:

Thesis statement:

Example of an Introduction Paragraph:

    When exactly is the right time to decide to end the suffering of a loved one? What does it take to make such a decision, and how would one ever truly know if he or she is justified in doing so? These are the questions faced by George Milton at the end of John Steinbeck's novella, *Of Mice and Men*. After a seemingly endless string of mishaps and misadventures, George's best friend, a mentally challenged giant by the name of Lennie Small, finally makes the innocent but fatal mistake of killing a woman at the ranch where they work. As the men of the ranch frantically try to bring Lennie to justice, probably by killing him in cold blood, George must decide whether to try to escape with Lennie, turn him over to the men or the law, or end Lennie's life quickly and peacefully himself. In the end, George makes the right decision in killing Lennie because _____, _____, and _____.

Figure 4.3. Graphic Organizer for Introductory Paragraph

10. Score the essays using a scoring guide for argument writing, such as the SBA scoring guide for argumentative writing or another argument-writing rubric.

The Crucible Performance Task

Special thanks to Sandy Graham and other colleagues who collaborated in designing this performance task. Arthur Miller's play *The Crucible* was inspired by Miller's own observations and experiences during the 1950s, a time of widespread fear of Communism and Communist infiltrators. The play is loosely based on the Salem Witch Trials of 1692 in Salem, Massachusetts, and the extreme hysteria that resulted. Miller observed several parallels between the Salem Witch Trials and the U.S. Senate Hearings led by Senator Joseph McCarthy in the 1950s that resulted in accusations against numerous people, including well-known Hollywood insiders, government officials, and authors. Arthur Miller was himself called before the Senate Committee and asked to provide testimony and name names, which he refused to do.

The play itself focuses on several young girls in the Puritan community of Salem who were caught in the woods supposedly performing black magic and conjuring the spirits of the dead. A whole series of accusations and desperate finger-pointing result as the girls try to avoid punishment by making accusations against innocent townspeople. The play dramatically portrays the mass paranoia and hysteria that engulfed the town and resulted in the execution of nineteen men and women by the end of 1692.

Miller's play stands as a strong warning against theocracy and the extremism and intolerance that it promotes. Miller was one of the most influential modern American playwrights, and this play presents a fascinating and riveting story. You may want to supplement reading of the play with viewing of the excellent 1996 film version of the play, starring Daniel Day Lewis and Winona Ryder.

You may also want to precede the reading of this play with instruction about some of the Puritan language and cultural references from the play. You might begin by teaching students the term "theocracy," which is a government based on a set of religious beliefs. Puritan New England functioned as a theocratic government, and *The Crucible*, in addition to being a compelling drama, is also Miller's warning against the dangers of theocracy. Also, there are various Puritan-era terms, such as "Goody" to refer to a woman, usually an older woman and one who is married; it is a shortened form of the term "Goodwife." For example, John Proctor's wife in the play is referred to as "Goody Proctor." Other terms used that you may want to pre-teach include the following:

- Poppet—a now-obsolete term for a doll
- Conjure—to call up or raise the spirits of the dead

- Covenanted—a person bound by God's laws or scriptural precepts
- Crucible—a container made of a metal capable of withstanding intense heat and used for melting metal and ores; it also means "a severe test or trial."
- Lechery—excessive sexual indulgence. The Puritans would have used this term to refer to any sexual misbehavior, including extramarital sex, or adultery, and behaving in an overtly sexual manner.

This performance task addresses the following standards:

- Reading Literature Standard 1: Cite strong and thorough textual evidence to support analysis of what the text says explicitly as well as inferences drawn from the text.
- Reading Literature Standard 2: Determine a theme or central idea of a text and analyze in detail its development over the course of the text, including how it emerges and is shaped and refined by specific detail.
- Writing Standard 1: Write arguments to support claims in an analysis of substantive topics or texts, using valid reasoning and relevant and sufficient evidence.

In addition to the text of the play itself, several other reading selections are recommended to prepare students for the essay they will be writing. They can also be used as pre-reading activities to build background knowledge about the time period and events that make up the setting and plot of the play. If the links to the articles provided here have changed, you should be able to find the articles with a simple Google search. Some of the selections may provide evidence for student essays, depending on which topic they choose:

- Cotton Mather, "The Trial of Martha Carrier" (you can find copies of this online) or another excerpt from Mather's *Wonders of the Invisible World*.
- The article "The Salem Witch Trials, 1692," http://www.eyewitnesstohistory.com/salem.htm.
- The article "A Brief History of the Salem Witch Trials," by Jess Blumberg, http://www.smithsonianmag.com/history/a-brief-history-of-the-salem-witch-trials-175162489/http://www.sm.
- The article "Ergotism: The Satan Loosed in Salem?" by Linda R. Caporael, *Science*, Vol. 192, April 2, 1976, http://www.sciencemag.org/content/192/4234/21.
- An article about McCarthyism of the 1950s. Choose one of the following two articles: 1. "McCarthyism" by Ellen Schrecker, *Dictionary of American History*, 2003, http://www.encyclopedia.com/topic/McCarthyism.aspx. 2. "McCarthyism," U.S. History website, http://www.ushistory.org/us/53a.asp.

Follow this lesson sequence for the performance task:

1. Conduct a class reading and/or dramatization of the play. Assign individual reading parts and conduct a guided reading of each act of the play. Between each act, have students work on study questions and do other brief activities before moving on to the next act. You might also intersperse the reading of the play with some of the other readings.
2. Upon completion of all the readings, you may want to conduct a Socratic Seminar or some other form of whole-group discussion. Students will need to understand the performance task assignment and choose one of the essay topics provided. Explain that the essay will be an argument essay in which they develop and present a claim, supporting it with textual evidence from the play and other reading selections. Their essay must introduce a precise claim, develop the claim with specific evidence, use transitional words and phrases to link sections of the essay, establish and maintain a formal writing style, and provide an effective conclusion.
3. Present the following essay topics to students, and ask them to choose the one they would like to write about:

   - What is an individual's responsibility to speak out against injustice and wrongdoing? Who should have spoken out more in the play? Why? Be sure to connect your ideas to specific characters and situations in the play.
   - Choose one character from *The Crucible*. Argue whether his or her actions throughout the play are selfish or sacrificial. Is he or she a hero or a villain? Why?
   - Consider what life was like in Puritan times. The government was a theocracy. Social standing was directly related to a person's position in the church. Consider why Proctor initially refuses to sign the confession. In the end, should he have torn up his confession and condemned himself to death, or should he have confessed to save his life? Explain your reasons with evidence.
   - Using evidence from one of the articles we read and the play itself, which theory (ergotism, fraud, medical reasons, hysteria, or encephalitis) do you believe is the true cause of the Salem Witch Trials?
   - Who do you think made the most ethical choices—Giles Corey, John Proctor, or Tituba? Support your claim with quotes and evidence from the play.
   - Arthur Miller wrote *The Crucible* in protest against McCarthyism. Did he do a good job of comparing the two? State your reasons, and support them with evidence from the play and the article on McCarthyism.
4. Have students complete a required brainstorming activity, which could include a T-chart, web, or diagram that includes their claim and support. Assign a grade for completion, and check the brainstorming activities to

make sure students are on the right track and prepared to begin writing the essay.
5. Present a list of common transitional words and phrases that students can refer to during their writing. Remind them that they need to include transitions between ideas and sections of their paper.
6. Have students complete the first draft of their paper and spend some time revising. You might want to have them submit their drafts to you for brief review or conduct individual conferences with students about their drafts. If you prefer, incorporate a peer review and response activity to allow students to read others' papers and provide suggestions for them. Students should spend at least a portion of one class period working on revising their drafts.
7. Have students prepare a final, typed draft of their essay. Follow some of the suggestions from the argument section in this chapter.
8. As a culminating activity, have students create a poster or visual of the ideas from their final draft and share them with a gallery walk. As an alternate activity, have students read their papers aloud in small groups.
9. These essays can be scored with the SBA argument-writing rubric. We use the SBA argument rubric approved by our district, which scores papers from 1 to 4 in the areas of Purpose and Focus, Organization, Elaboration of Evidence, Language and Vocabulary, and Conventions.

Ricochet River Performance Task

Robin Cody is a well-known Oregon writer, and his novel *Ricochet River* is a recipient of the Oregon Book Award. It has been compared to such classics as *Catcher in the Rye* because of its adolescent appeal. The story is set in a fictional town called Calamus, Oregon, in the 1960s and focuses on three teenagers and their dreams: Wade is very athletic; his friend Jesse is Native American; and Wade's girlfriend, Lorna, longs to leave the small town behind. This story is very appealing to adolescent readers as a coming-of-age story, and it also blends in a great deal of Oregon and Native American history.

First, some discussion of the setting and history: Set in the beautiful Columbia River Gorge, just east of the Cascade Mountains of northwestern Oregon, Celilo Falls was at one time the sixth-largest waterfall in the world. The Columbia River separates Washington and Oregon, and for centuries, local Native American tribes, such as the Umatilla, Warm Springs, and Nez Perce, gathered at Celilo Falls to fish, catching salmon with their nets and spears. Celilo Falls was also a center of activity for the Native American tribes and served as a trading post, even for tribes who came from thousands of miles away. It is thought to be the oldest continuously inhabited community anywhere in North America.

When white settlers began to arrive in the area and settle in communities to the east of the falls, great changes began, and by 1940, the area had grown rapidly. Eventually, a huge dam was built on the Columbia to provide power to the area, facilitate river navigation, and provide irrigation water for farmland. A previous treaty had guaranteed that local tribes could continue fishing in Celilo Falls, but of course, with the building of the Dalles Dam, the great Celilo Falls was submerged and ceased to exist. Local tribes never received the government compensation money they were promised after the dam was built. In *Ricochet River*, the character Jesse engages in a process of discovering his own native ancestry.

This performance task was designed by my colleague Cara Fortey. It asks students to research the historical issues the novel raises and then write an argumentative essay. Unlike the other performance tasks, all students write on the same topic. Bear in mind that this novel does have content and language that may be questionable for some readers, so consider your local community standards before using it in the classroom. It has been banned in some communities, even here in Oregon, although overall, it has been quite popular since it is written by a local author and focuses on a local setting.

This performance task addresses the following standard:

- Writing Standard 1: Write arguments to support claims in an analysis of substantive topics or texts, using valid reasoning and relevant and sufficient evidence.

In addition to the book itself, there are several other texts, literary and informational, print and visual, included for students to study in preparation for writing the essay:

- Celilo Falls pictures: http://www.oldoregonphotos.com/location/celilo-falls.html (a series of twenty-three historic photographs)
- "Salmon Mashup: Rare Celilo Falls Film & Radio Chronicle," https://www.youtube.com/watch?v=EfqL5_2sMwM
- "Celilo Falls, Oregon—1956," https://www.youtube.com/watch?v=u7XBFHry4VQ. This is a ten-minute film that shows net fishing at Celilo Falls.
- "Columbia River Inter-Tribal Fish Commission: Celilo Falls (with newsreel), http://www.critfc.org/salmon-culture/tribal-salmon-culture/celilo-falls/. This article, which includes a newsreel, presents the Celilo Falls controversy from the Native American point of view.

- "Northwest Power and Conservation Council: Celilo Falls," http://www.nwcouncil.org/history/CeliloFalls. This historical account presents the views of the power industry on the Celilo Falls controversy.
- The poem "Dreaming of Celilo Falls: A Poem of Resurrection and Reclaiming," http://friendsofcelilofalls.wordpress.com/2012/11/20/dreaming-of-celilo-falls-a-poem-of-resurrection-and-reclaiming/
- The poem "Celilo Falls," by Jessica Minier Mabe, 1992, http://jessicaminiermabe.wordpress.com/2011/12/17/poem-of-the-day-celilo-falls/. This poem is based on a story the poet's mother told her about going to Celilo Falls to fish for salmon.
- The poem "Tsagaglalal: She Who Watches," by David Hedges, originally published in *The Oregonian* and then in a local collection called *Honoring Our Rivers*. Available at www.david.hedges.name/poems/tsagaglalal-she-who-watches.

Follow this lesson sequence for the performance task:

1. After completion of the whole-class reading and discussion of *Ricochet River*, have students complete their study of all the other selections: poems, informational texts, and videos. Have students take Cornell Notes during their reading and viewing, which will help provide them with evidence to support their essays.
2. As an optional activity, engage the class in a Socratic Seminar or other form of discussion following their reading and viewing of all the supplementary texts.
3. Next, tell students they will be writing an argument paper about the Celilo Falls controversy. Explain that in their essay, they will need to draw on textual evidence from *Ricochet River* and the other sources and that all essays must include the following items: a precise claim, specific evidence and examples, transitional words and phrases to link major sections, a formal writing style, and an effective conclusion.
4. Present the following essay prompt to students: Authorities are considering removing the Dalles Dam and restoring Celilo Falls. Write an argumentative essay explaining why you agree or disagree with this idea. Support your claim with evidence from what you have read and viewed. (Note: In recent years, there have been movements in support of removing the dam and restoring the original falls. Removal of the dam, while possible, is perhaps unrealistic because, as the area has grown up around the Columbia River, removing the dam would completely flood many communities downstream of the current dam. If you wish, you could change the prompt to something like the following: "Write an argument essay

arguing that building of the Dalles Dam in 1957 was or was not a good decision. Consider the benefits of the dam as well as its effects on the lives, traditions, and culture of the Native Americans."
5. Have students complete a pre-writing activity for their essay, such as a brainstorming, diagram, graphic organizer, list, or free write. Assign a grade for completion of the pre-writing.
6. Have students prepare an outline of their essay, with the claim statement clearly written at the top. Have students turn in the outline for a checkpoint grade and review the claim statements, making sure that students have a clear and supportable argumentative claim.
7. Present a list of common transitions that students can refer to during their writing. Remind them that they need to include transitions between ideas and sections of their paper.
8. Have students write the first draft of their paper. Present a rubric or checklist for them to use during revision. Incorporate a peer response activity to allow students to read others' papers and provide suggestions. If you wish, use the response form for argument writing provided in this chapter.
9. Have students prepare a final, typed copy of their essay. As a culminating activity, have students share excerpts of their paper with the whole class or in small groups. As an alternative activity, students might use their essays to create a one-pager about Celilo Falls and their argument (see the one-pager strategy description in Chapter Two).
10. Score these essays using a scoring guide for argument writing. We use the SBA argument-writing rubric approved by our district, which scores the paper from 1 to 4 in the areas of Purpose and Focus, Organization, Elaboration of Evidence, Language and Vocabulary, and Conventions.

The Bean Trees Performance Task

Barbara Kingsolver's novel *The Bean Trees* is one of our teachers' favorite books to teach. The endearing characters and meaningful themes are combined with Kingsolver's humorous and colorful writing style, and students respond positively to this book. The book features Taylor Greer, a spirited and headstrong young woman who leaves her native small town in Kentucky to avoid the same fate as all the other young girls of her town: getting pregnant and living in poverty. Taylor describes herself early in the novel as "the one to get away."

Ill-equipped to deal with the world on her own, Taylor struggles at first but eventually ends up in Tucson, Arizona, where she is able to find a couple of good friends and a job. Ironically, she also ends up as the adoptive parent to a young Native American girl whom she names Turtle, a child who was abandoned and left in Taylor's care. Taylor must find a way to take care of herself as well as a small child, and she finds many invaluable friends along the way. The novel features several powerful themes, dealing head-on with issues such as illegal immigration; child abuse; discrimination; and more positively, resilience, family, parenthood, friendship, and the interdependence of human beings.

As noted, in *The Bean Trees*, immigration is one of the major themes. This performance task asks students to consider how the issue is presented in the novel and also to read several supplementary texts that present both sides of the immigration debate. Students will then be asked to construct their own argument essay on the topic. This performance task was designed by my colleague Matthew Isom, with some additional material added to the original.

This performance task addresses the following standards:

- Reading Literature Standard 2: Determine a theme or central idea of a text and analyze in detail its development over the course of the text, including how it emerges and is shaped and refined by specific details; provide an objective summary of the text.
- Writing Standard 1: Write arguments to support claims in an analysis of substantive topics or texts, using valid reasoning and relevant and sufficient evidence.

In addition to the novel itself, there are several editorials and readings on the topic of immigration reform. Some of them are focused on the debate regarding the 2013 Immigration Reform Bill, and some are more recent. As of this writing, the country's new president and his administration have again thrust the immigration debate into the spotlight, with his calls for banning Muslim immigrants, deporting those without legal citizenship, and building a wall on the U.S.-Mexico border. No immigration reform bill has been passed by Congress as of this writing. You may want to add to and update the list of readings provided here, perhaps including sources more relevant to current circumstances for this most-controversial topic. You might also select from among the readings, depending on your particular group of students. In case the provided links do not work, most of these texts can easily be found with an Internet search:

- "Don't Fear the Immigrants," by Leonard Pitts Jr., *The Spokesman Review*, Saturday, April 1, 2006, http://www.spokesman.com/stories/2006/apr/01/leonard-pitts-jr-dont-fear-the-immigrants/
- "Trump's Comments Echo Party Line," by Leonard Pitts Jr., *Miami Herald*, July 7, 2015, http://www.miamiherald.com/opinion/opn-columns-blogs/leonard-pitts-jr/article26705164.html

Performance Tasks Designed for Specific Literary Texts 127

- Video: "State of the Union 2014 Address: Obama Urges Immigration Reform," *New York Times*, http://www.youtube.com/watch?v=Cvs-JZqaqwo
- Immigration Bill Summary, by the Associated Press, June 28, 2013, http://www.politico.com/story/2013/06/immigration-bill-summary-093557
- "The Case for the Border Fence," by David Horowitz, *Conservative Review* (online), August 25, 2015, http://www.conservativereview.com/commentary/2015/08/border-fences-work. This article contains great graphs, charts, and photographs.
- "Humanity? Practicality? Amnesty? The Arguments for and Against Immigration Reform," by Carrie Dann, NBC News, Friday, April 12, 2013, http://nbcpolitics.nbcnews.com/_news/2013/04/12/17707895-humanity-practicality-amnesty-the-arguments-for-and-against-immigration-reform?lite
- "Five Reasons Obama Shouldn't Declare Amnesty," by David Frum, November 17, 2014, *The Atlantic*, http://www.theatlantic.com/politics/archive/2014/11/five-reasons-obama-shouldnt-declare-amnesty-immigration-executive-order/382845/
- Alabama Senator Denies the Moral Responsibility of Immigration Reform," by Janelle Tupper, *Sojourners*, March 21, 2013, https://sojo.net/articles/alabama-senator-denies-moral-responsibility-immigration-reform
- "Sen. Jeff Sessions: Trump Is Right on Muslim Immigration Ban," by Elise Cooper, *American Thinker*, June 22, 2016, http://www.americanthinker.com/articles/2016/06/sen_jeff_sessions_trump_is_right_on_muslim_immigration_ban.html
- Republican Stance on Immigration, http://www.republicanviews.org/republican-views-on-immigration/
- Democratic Stance on Immigration, https://www.democrats.org/party-platform-broken-immigration
- "Can Congress Act? Dolan Stresses Human, Moral Costs of Inaction," by Kevin Clark, *America: The National Catholic Review*, November 25, 2013, http://americamagazine.org/issue/can-congress-act-dolan-stresses-human-moral-costs-inaction/

Follow this lesson sequence for the performance task, following reading of the novel:

1. Present the following information to students to help frame the performance task assignment and topic:
   "The Immigration Bill of 2013 was passed by the U.S. Senate but failed to pass in the House of Representatives, and although President Obama supported comprehensive immigration reform, no congressional action

on immigration has happened to date. President Trump campaigned on the promise of stopping illegal immigration and has cracked down on illegal immigrants by stepping up deportation of those who have committed crimes. The dilemma facing the government is just what to do about the eleven million undocumented immigrants currently living in this country as well as future undocumented immigrants. For many decades, Americans have struggled to find an appropriate and effective response to this reality. Leonard Pitts Jr., of the *Miami Herald*, says that to intelligently deal with a complex issue like this, we must "surmount one of the least attractive traits of the American character. Meaning a preference for responding to complicated questions with simplistic answers." The reasons that people choose simplistic answers to problems is that it is easier to do so. To make informed decisions takes thought, research, and critical thinking. This is the task before us. The issue of immigration is dealt with extensively in Kingsolver's novel *The Bean Trees*, where we hear the character Mattie say, "We have a moral responsibility to help those who come to this country." In the context of the novel, the people have come "fleeing for their lives" from the civil-war-torn country of Guatemala, and they desperately need help. The primary question that the novel presents us with is, "What are we going to do when we encounter people in need?" Arguments have been raised in recent years concerning possible legislation on immigration. Presidential candidates have also shared their policy positions on immigration reform. Attorney General Jeff Sessions has said that we have "no moral or legal responsibility to reward somebody who entered the country illegally." President Donald Trump has stated that all illegal immigrants must be deported, and he has vowed to build a wall on the U.S.-Mexico border. Others disagree. President Barack Obama and presidential candidate Hillary Clinton both support comprehensive immigration reform that provides a path to citizenship. Cardinal Dolan, in 2013, stated that "this is a matter of great moral urgency that cannot wait any longer for action."

2. Next, present students with the essay prompt "Consider the issue of immigration as presented in the novel and other readings, and write an argumentative essay answering the question 'Do we have a moral responsibility to help illegal immigrants and, if so, in what ways?' Base your answer on several examples and pieces of evidence from *The Bean Trees* as well as evidence from the other reading selections. Your essay must include the following: a precise claim, specific evidence, transitional words and phrases to link major sections, a formal writing style, and an effective conclusion."

3. Present students with the supplementary reading selections and have them take Cornell Notes. You may want to schedule a discussion, a Socratic Seminar, or other activities after reading the supplementary articles.

4. Have students complete a pre-writing activity for their essay, such as a brainstorming, diagram, cluster, graphic organizer, list, or free write. Assign a grade for completion of the pre-writing.
5. Have students prepare an outline of their paper with the claim statement clearly written at the top. Have students turn in the outline for an additional checkpoint grade, and review the claim statements carefully, making suggestions for revision if necessary. Preparing an outline will help students more effectively organize their evidence and incorporate transitions.
6. Provide students with a list of common transitional words and phrases they can refer to during their writing. Remind them that their essay needs to include transitions between ideas and sections of their paper.
7. Have students write the first draft of their paper and spend some time revising. Present a rubric or checklist for them to use during revision. You may want to incorporate a peer response activity to allow students to read others' papers and provide suggestions.
8. Have students prepare a final, typed draft of their essay.
9. Culminating activity: Have students share their essays by reading an excerpt of their paper to the class or discussing their essays in small groups. Another alternative is to organize a class debate or Philosophical Chairs activity on the topic of whether we have a moral responsibility to help illegal immigrants.
10. These essays can be scored using the SBA argument-writing rubric, which scores the papers from 1 to 4 in the areas of Purpose and Focus, Organization, Elaboration of Evidence, Language and Vocabulary, and Conventions.

The House on Mango Street Performance Task

The House on Mango Street is a beautiful, poetic novella by Latina writer Sandra Cisneros. Published in 1984, it presents a series of vignettes told by the main character, Esperanza Cordero. The novel is a coming-of-age story that covers a year of Esperanza's life, beginning with her family's move into a house on Mango Street in a crowded Latino neighborhood in Chicago. The vignettes function as short stories and tell of Esperanza's struggle toward maturity. Her journey includes good friends and happy memories as well as painful encounters with poverty, sexism, and abuse.

Esperanza's central internal conflict is her anxiety over her family's poverty, but over the course of the novel, she learns to accept her situation and resolve that someday she can escape and have a home of her own, a home of her dreams. Esperanza begins writing to express herself and to escape from the poverty and despair of the neighborhood. The novel's vignettes also tell the story of many of Esperanza's neighbors, many of whom become influential to her growth and maturity.

Esperanza grows from being an insecure young child to a confident young woman: "One day I will pack my bags of books and paper. One day I will say goodbye to Mango. I am too strong for her to keep me here forever." She also comes to understand that, as one of the other characters tells her, "You will always be Esperanza. You will always be Mango Street. You can't erase what you know. You can't forget who you are."

This performance task asks students to write an expository essay that focuses on one of the novel's central themes. It addresses the following standards:

- Reading Literature Standard 1: Cite strong and thorough textual evidence to support analysis of what the text says explicitly as well as inferences drawn from the text.
- Reading Literature Standard 2: Determine a theme or central idea of a text and analyze in detail its development over the course of the text, including how it emerges and is shaped and refined by specific detail.
- Writing Standard 2. Write informative/explanatory texts to examine and convey complex ideas, concepts, and information clearly and accurately through effective selection, organization, and analysis of content.

Students will be using the novel itself to gather evidence to support their thesis statement; in addition, you can select from the following reading selections (and one video), from which students can draw evidence for their essays. The selections not referenced with a web address are available through common academic databases, and the last three are published in the book by Heyck (1994):

- Reader Commentary from the Artifice, February 20, 2014, "The House on Mango Street: An Illustration of Machismo," http://the-artifice.com/the-house-on-mango-street-machismo/
- Sandra Hughes Hassell and Sandy L. Guild, 2002, "The Urban Experience in Recent Young Adult Novels," *The ALAN Review*, Vol. 29, No. 3, http://scholar.lib.vt.edu/ejournals/ALAN/v29n3/hassell.html
- Video: "The House on Mango Street—The Story," April 2, 2009, https://www.youtube.com/watch?v=0Pyf89VsNmg&t=230s. Sandra Cisneros talks about the novel and its connections to her own life and experience.
- Amy Sickles, 2010, "The Critical Reception of *The House on Mango Street*," book chapter from *Critical Insights: The House on Mango Street*, pp. 36–55, Salem Press.
- Randy Ribay, 2013, "What Makes a Good YA Urban Novel?" *Horn Book Magazine*, Vol. 89, No. 6, pp. 48–53.

- JoAnn Balingit, 1995, "The House on Mango Street," *Masterplots II: Women's Literature Series*, pp. 1–3.
- Interview with Jesus Martinez and Ricardo Murillo, from the book *Barrios and Borderlands: Cultures of Latinos and Latinas in the United States*, by Denis Lynn Daly Heyck (1994). This interview presents the stories of two immigrants and their experiences.
- Excerpt from *Bless Me, Ultima*, by Rudolfo Anaya. The excerpt from Anaya's novel depicts the narrator, Tony, experiencing his first day of school and deals with themes of identity and assimilation of Latinos. The excerpt is included in the book *Barrios and Borderlands* (Heyck, 1994).
- Interview with Father Jerome Martinez, also from the book *Barrios and Borderlands* (Heyck, 1994). This interview features Father Martinez's description of the state of New Mexico, its Latino culture and Latinos' characteristics.

Follow this lesson sequence for the performance task:

1. Have students complete their reading of the whole novel. Because of the brief, yet poetic nature of the book's segments, several of the vignettes you may want to read aloud with students. You might assign each student to read aloud one vignette for the class, giving him or her time to practice his or her oral reading. Include discussion and activities as the class proceeds through the reading.
2. Present students with the following essay prompt: "Most of the vignettes included in the book are short and may seem disconnected, yet taken as a whole, the book does develop and focus on several important themes. Choose one of the following themes, and write an expository essay that traces how the theme is developed throughout the course of the book. Use evidence from the book itself as well as the other reading selection included. The themes are racism and prejudice, poverty, gender roles, domestic violence, growing up/coming of age, culture and environment, family."
3. After students have had a chance to think about the prompt, spend some time focusing on the literary element of theme, and review how authors develop themes. Make sure students understand the difference between plot and theme, that theme is not what happens but rather the underlying meaning of a literary work. While a subject is the topic the author writes about, the theme expresses a statement or opinion about the subject, and it may be largely implicit. Also, authors can express themes directly through narrative commentary, thoughts and conversations of the characters, the characters and their experiences, and the story's action and events. Ask students to give some examples of each of these methods from *The House on Mango Street*.

4. Give students a few index cards to use for their initial note taking. Ask them to identify five vignettes or segments in the novel that can provide evidence for the theme they have chosen. Have them re-read the vignettes carefully and then use a separate note card to write down notes and evidence from that vignette that they will be able to use in their essay. Some of their evidence should be quotations from the vignettes they will want to use in their essay.
5. Next, have students read and take notes on the supplementary readings. They can use additional index cards to take notes from the readings that will provide further evidence and support for their essay.
6. After students have finished reading, re-reading, and note taking, have them write a thesis statement for their essay. For example, "*The House on Mango Street* illustrates Cisneros's belief that our culture and environment shape and develop us and become part of who we are as individuals and that we cannot leave our past behind." Another example: "Several characters and incidents in the novel *House on Mango Street* demonstrate the unfair and abusive situations women are placed in because of their gender." Check students' thesis statements and offer them suggestions for revising.
7. Using their thesis statement and notes as a starting point, have students complete the first draft of their paper. It might be important here to conduct a mini-lesson to show students how to correctly integrate quotations and source material into their essays. Explain that each quote must be introduced and integrated into the writer's own sentences, not just dropped into the essay. Share some examples and show students how to do this. You should require them to cite the page number of the quotes at the end of each quote. If possible, have them submit their first draft to you for a brief review, or conduct a peer response activity so that students can provide some suggestions for improving each other's papers.
8. Have students spend some time revising their essays. Provide a list of common transition words and phrases that students can refer to during their revising. Have them check to make sure appropriate transitions are used between sections of their papers.
9. Have students prepare a final, typed draft of their essay.
10. As a culminating activity, have students share their papers in small groups. Also, have students create a one-pager (see Chapter Two) focusing on the five vignettes from the book they originally chose to use for evidence. Their one-pager should include quotes from the vignettes and meet the other requirements of the one-pager. Have students display their one-pagers and share them with a gallery walk.

11. The essays can be scored using any scoring guide for informative/expository writing.

Poetry Performance Tasks

This section includes two separate performance tasks focusing on poetry: one is a theme-based comparison project, and the other is a layered curriculum activity. Poetry is an important genre of literature, and it is important for students to learn about poetic elements and techniques as well as to analyze and critique poetry, which these tasks promote.

Part One: Literary Analysis of Theme

This first task asks students to read two poems with a common theme or motif and then complete a literary analysis activity to compare them. The sample task here asks students to write about two poems dealing with the subject of death, but you can use this same task for any two poems that have some common topical or thematic elements. You could choose poems from a similar era, poems that focus on a common theme, or poems that present contrasting views and themes.

This performance task addresses the following standards:

- Reading Literature Standard 1: Cite strong and thorough textual evidence to support analysis of what the text says explicitly as well as inferences drawn from the text.
- Reading Literature Standard 2: Determine a theme or central idea of a text and analyze in detail its development over the course of the text, including how it emerges and is shaped and refined by specific details.
- Reading Literature Standard 4: Determine the meaning of words and phrases as they are used in the text, including figurative and connotative meanings; analyze the cumulative impact of specific word choices on meaning and tone.
- Writing Standard 2: Write informative/explanatory texts to examine and convey complex ideas, concepts, and information clearly and accurately through the effective selection, organization, and analysis of content.
- Writing Standard 4: Produce clear and coherent writing in which the development, organization, and style are appropriate to task, purpose, and audience.
- Language Standard 5: Demonstrate understanding of figurative language, word relationships, and nuances in word meanings.

If you choose to have students complete this comparative literary analysis task for two poems about death, you can choose from among the following classic poems that deal with the subject. You may want to choose two that take similar stances on the subject, or you may want to choose two that have opposing themes or stances, perhaps one that is dark and heavy and one that presents a more positive view. You might even prefer to choose two poems on a common theme by the same poet. Here are some possibilities for poems that deal with the topic of death:

- "If I Should Die," by Emily Dickinson
- "Because I Could Not Stop for Death," by Emily Dickinson
- "Death Be Not Proud," by John Milton
- "Thanatopsis," by Oliver Wendell Holmes
- "Do Not Go Gentle into That Good Night," by Dylan Thomas
- "Transfiguration," by Louisa May Alcott
- "I Felt a Funeral in my Brain," by Emily Dickinson
- "Only Death," by Pablo Neruda
- "And You as Well Must Die," by Edna St. Vincent Millay
- "Annabel Lee," by Edgar Allan Poe
- "Crossing the Bar," by Alfred Lord Tennyson
- "Death," by Rainer Maria Rilke
- "Do Not Stand at my Grave and Weep," by Mary Elizabeth Frye
- "The Reaper and the Flowers," by Henry Wadsworth Longfellow
- "When I am Dead, My Dearest," by Christina Rossetti
- "A Happy Man," by Edwin Arlington Robinson
- "Life," by Charlotte Bronte
- "On Another's Sorrow," by William Blake
- "To an Athlete Dying Young," by A. E. Housman
- "Remember," by Christina Rossetti
- "O Captain! My Captain!" by Walt Whitman

Follow this procedure for completing the performance task:

1. Present students with the following prompt: "Read the two poems provided. Consider how both writers present the topic of death, and write an essay that compares and contrasts their ideas about death. Consider each poem's style and the ways in which the theme is developed throughout the poem. Include specific evidence from the poems in your analysis."
2. Make sure students fully understand the prompt by having them underline the key words and directions in the prompt itself that point out what they need to do in their essays.
3. Next, provide students with a copy of both poems that they can mark. You may want to begin by reading the two poems aloud with students. Then use the text-marking strategy from Chapter Two, having students carefully

read and mark the text, noting stylistic elements, examples of figurative language, word choices, and thematic elements in the two poems.
4. Next, ask students to write a thesis statement for their essay. They need to make sure that their thesis statement is clear and precise and states their main point about how the two poems are similar or different. Emphasize for students that in writing, poem titles are always placed in quotation marks. Check students' thesis statements, and make necessary suggestions for revision. Check to be sure students have identified, by title and author, both poems in their thesis statements.
5. For a pre-writing activity, have students complete a Venn diagram or a T-chart as a way of noting similarities and differences between the two poems.
6. Next, have students complete an outline of their essay. Explain that there are two methods of organizing a comparison-contrast essay: the one-side-at-a-time method and the point-by-point method. For the first method, students would focus on analyzing one poem in the first half of their paper and then focus on the other poem for the second half. The point-by-point method, which may be preferable for this task, would present a number of points of comparison, each in a separate paragraph, and discuss each poem in turn. You may want to provide an outline template, such as the following, to help students visualize the organization:

Introduction

Thesis statement
  I. First point of comparison
    A. Poem 1
    B. Poem 2
  II. Second point of comparison
    A. Poem 1
    B. Poem 2
  III. Third point of comparison
    A. Poem 1
    B. Poem 2
  IV. Fourth point of comparison
    A. Poem 1
    B. Poem 2
  V. Fifth point of comparison
    A. Poem 1
    B. Poem 2
  VI. Conclusion

7. After students have completed an outline, they should write the first draft of the essay. Provide students with a list of transitional words and phrases to refer to during writing.

8. Have students spend some time revising their writing. Present a rubric or checklist, such as the following:

- Do I have an interesting introduction that includes the titles of both poems?
- Is my thesis statement clear?
- Am I using appropriate language and word choice and maintaining a formal style?
- Have I included specific examples from each poem to support my points, in every paragraph?
- Is the essay well organized and easy to follow?
- Have I used transitional words and phrases to connect my ideas?
- Does the conclusion paragraph restate the thesis in a different way?
- Does the essay have a conclusion that brings the essay to a satisfying ending?

You may want to incorporate a peer response activity to allow students to read others' papers and provide suggestions.
9. Have students prepare a final, typed draft of their essays. As a culminating activity, have students share their essays by reading them aloud in small groups.
10. Score the essays using a scoring guide for informational/explanatory writing. The scoring guide or rubric might include the following categories: ideas and content, organization, use of textual evidence, language and style, and conventions.

Part Two: Layered Curriculum

This second poetry task is one that many teachers have used successfully. It is not a traditional performance task, and it is not tied to specific standards, although it can be used to meet a number of different standards. Some have criticized the CCSS for neglecting learning styles and multiple intelligences in their design. This task is one that allows for multiple Common Core Standards to be addressed but also allows students to capitalize on their individual learning styles and multiple intelligences. The task is a layered curriculum activity for poetry that provides students with a lot of choices and freedom. It provides built-in differentiation so students can choose activities better suited to their range of abilities. It also allows them to choose what grade they want to earn by choosing from among several tasks and activities that require different depths of study.

Kathie Nunley designed the layered curriculum approach as an innovative teaching strategy in the 1980s (Colding, 2016). The layered curriculum "builds on students' varied learning styles and multiple intelligences (linguistic, logical-mathematical, spatial, bodily-kinesthetic, musical, interpersonal, intrapersonal, or naturalistic) in ways that help students make meaning of academic content" (Colding, 2016, p. 1). Students are allowed to choose activities that best fit their learning needs and styles, instead of every student completing the same activity. Colding (2016) notes that it is a good strategy for motivating students and creating a learner-centered classroom.

Layered curriculum involves creating three layers of activities: the C level, B level, and A level. The C level presents students with several assignment choices that cover the general or basic content requirements. For students who wish to advance to the B level, they must rely on knowledge they learned from the C level and apply the concepts learned. The top level, A level, requires students to engage in a higher level of critical thinking. Students choose one activity from a number of choices, using higher-order thinking skills and using knowledge gained from the two lower levels (Colding, 2016).

The project allows the teacher to serve as a facilitator rather than using direct instruction. You can circulate, talking with students about their work, providing suggestions, and helping students find appropriate resources. With the layered curriculum, students are self-directed, choosing not only which activities they will complete, but also what grade they will receive, which depends on how many of the layers they complete.

Follow the procedure here for the layered curriculum for poetry:

1. Begin by gathering several poetry collections, preferably those that include many different poets, from different eras, styles, and nationalities. Enlist the aid of your librarian or media specialist to help you gather several poetry collections. During the layered curriculum task, keep the poetry books on a cart or in a designated space in your classroom. This activity will take several class periods to complete. You will want to specify a final completion date so students can plan ahead and use their time wisely.
2. Gather some additional materials and resources. In addition to the poetry collections, have students use an "Introduction to Poetry" section in their textbook as reference (or make available an article from a textbook or other source that provides an overview of poetry study). Also, find an appropriate video on poetry, and make it available for students who might want to choose a particular task using the video. You might also have available copies of literary handbooks or lists of poetry terms with definitions. Also, you will need a collection of magazines and newspapers that students can cut up for specific activities. Some students may also need to do library research to complete certain activities, particularly at the higher level, so having a set of laptops or Chromebooks or a nearby computer lab may be helpful. Also, if you choose to include C-layer activity 1, you will need to create some mini-lectures on various aspects of poetry, such as

poem types, rhyme and rhythm, figurative language, imagery, symbolism and allegory, sound devices, and tone.
3. Hand out the Layered Curriculum Unit for Poetry assignment sheet (figure 4.4). Make sure that students understand that the A, B, and C levels will

---

LAYERED CURRICULUM POETRY UNIT

C-Layer:

Complete SIX of the following, one of which must be number 1, 2 or 3:

1. Listen to the daily mini-lectures on poetry and take outline notes. You will be expected to explain what you learned from the lectures.
2. Watch the video on poetry and take notes on types of poetry and poets included. You will be expected to explain what you learned from the video.
3. Read the "Introduction to Poetry" section in the textbook (or provided by the instructor) and write a one-page summary.
4. Read several poems from one of the poetry collections provided, and write a few discussion questions for at least five of them.
5. Choose a poem from one of the collections that you especially like and make a poetry poster that displays the poem and illustrates its poetic elements. The poster needs to include some color and other visual elements.
6. Make a set of twenty flashcards of poetry terminology.
7. Choose two poems from one or more collections that are similar and write a one-page comparison of the two.
8. Participate in a group reading and discussion of at least three poems. Read the poems out loud in the group and then have each group member share some points of analysis and things they noticed about each poem.
9. Write a poem of your own, with a minimum of fifteen lines, that follows a specific rhyme scheme and rhythm.
10. Choose a poem from one of the poetry collections. Research the author and read several other poems by that poet. Write a one-page essay that summarizes the major characteristics of that poet's work.
11. Write one of the following types of poems: ode, sonnet, animal poem, biopoem. Be prepared to explain your reasons for the poetic choices you made in the poem.
12. Use magazines and newspapers to create a Found Poem. Follow the instructions on the Found Poem Assignment Sheet.
13. Choose a poem with a minimum of 20 lines and prepare an oral reading for the instructor. Include discussion and evaluation of the poem.

B-Layer:

Choose ONE of the following options in addition to six of the C-layer options:

1. Using the poetry collections, choose a theme or topic and make a poetry collection that includes five poems, some visuals or illustrations, and an introduction that discusses the theme or topic in relation to the poems included.
2. Write three poems of your own and prepare an oral reading of them. Each poem must be a different type. Choose from among the following: ode, sonnet, narrative, series of haiku, villanelle, ballad, diamante, biopoem, rap, etc.

Figure 4.4. Layered Curriculum Poetry Unit

A-Layer:

Choose one of the following projects to complete in addition to six of the C-layer topics:

1. Do online research to explore the role of poetry in the modern world. For example, you might research the poetry of war, environmental poetry, poetry and the internet, poetry of race, children's poetry, feminist poetry, social protest/social justice poetry, etc. Search in magazines and websites that publish poetry. Write an essay of three pages which explains the role of poetry in the modern world as related to the particular current topic. In your essay, incorporate excerpts from the poetry examples you have found. Follow correct MLA format for quoting lines of poetry.
2. Choose several modern songs that have poetic elements. Type out the lyrics of each song or create a Powerpoint presentation for the class that presents recordings of the songs, discusses the poetic elements, and analyzes their themes and ideas. Include discussion of five or more different poetic elements. Focus the presentation on similarities between poetry and song. For the final part of the presentation, choose a poem from one of the collections provided and write music to match the lyrics. Play or sing the lyrics for the class, in person or in recorded format.

Figure 4.4. *(continued)*

correspond with the grade they will receive for the unit. If they complete only the C-layer activities, they will earn a C. To earn a B, they must complete level C plus one of the B-layer options. To earn an A, they must complete the C layer, plus one of the A-layer options.

4. You will also need a grade book or spreadsheet on which you can clearly mark which activities from which layers students complete during the unit.

The Poverty Performance Task

This final performance task is different from the previous ones in that it is not tied to a specific anchor text. This task was designed a few years ago for AVID students. We noticed that students often made disparaging and insensitive comments about people living in poverty, and since part of the AVID mission is to teach students to appreciate the value of community service, we realized they needed to learn more about some of the issues surrounding poverty and about those individuals and families who are socioeconomically disadvantaged.

While this task began as a research paper assignment with a community service component, literary selections were later added. There are many benefits to connecting the project to one or more literary texts that deal with the topic of poverty. While the primary goal was for students to learn some research skills, such as how to access source material using databases, how to synthesize information from various sources, and how to cite sources using MLA style, a secondary goal was to engage students in reading and discussion of literary text. Guest speakers were also brought into class to address the topic of poverty. The task provides students with real-world experience and an opportunity to participate in community service activities with an organization that works to combat poverty and hunger.

Overall, this project had a powerful result in terms of raising the consciousness of students on the issue of poverty and teaching students the importance of empathy.

This performance task addresses the following standards:

- Reading Literature Standard 1: Cite strong and thorough textual evidence to support analysis of what the text says explicitly as well as inferences drawn from the text.
- Reading Informational Text Standard 2: Determine a central idea of a text and analyze its development over the course of the text, including how it emerges and is shaped and refined by specific details; provide an objective summary of the text.
- Reading Informational Text Standard 6: Determine an author's point of view or purpose and analyze how an author uses rhetoric to advance that point of view or purpose.
- Writing Standard 4: Produce clear and coherent writing in which the development, organization, and style are appropriate to the task, purpose, and audience.
- Writing Standard 7: Conduct short as well as more sustained research projects to answer a question or solve a problem; narrow or broaden the inquiry when appropriate; synthesize multiple sources on the subject, demonstrating understanding of the subject under investigation.
- Writing Standard 8: Gather relevant information from multiple authoritative print and digital sources, using advanced searches effectively; assess the usefulness of each source in answering the research question; integrate information into the text selectively to maintain the flow of ideas, avoiding plagiarism and following a standard form for citation.
- Speaking and Listening Standard 2: Integrate multiple sources of information presented in diverse media or formats evaluating the credibility and accuracy of each source.

There are several possible literary selections you can choose from as anchor texts for this performance task. Even short children's books could be used effectively. Here is a general list of literary selections as well as a separate list of children's and adolescents' literature. You may think of others to add.

Possible literary selections:

- *Grapes of Wrath*, by John Steinbeck
- *Angela's Ashes*, by Frank McCourt
- *The Glass Castle*, by Jeannette Walls
- *A Tree Grows in Brooklyn*, by Betty Smith
- *The Absolutely True Diary of a Part-Time Indian*, by Sherman Alexie
- *Winter's Bone*, by Daniel Woodrell
- *The Jungle*, by Upton Sinclair
- *Make Lemonade*, by Virginia Euwer Wolff
- *The Bluest Eye*, by Toni Morrison
- *The Good Earth*, by Pearl S. Buck

Children's and adolescents' works:

- *Fly Away Home*, by Eve Bunting
- *December*, by Eve Bunting
- *Angel City*, by Tony Johnston and Carol Byard
- *Miracle's Boys*, by Jacqueline Woodson
- *The Hundred Dresses*, by Eleanor Estes
- *A Shelter in Our Car*, by Monica Gunning
- *Trash*, by Andy Mulligan
- *Sold*, by Patricia McCormick
- *The Hunger Games*, by Suzanne Collins
- *A Hero Ain't Nothin' but a Sandwich*, by Alice Childress

Begin by presenting students with the following overview of the performance task: "In the course of this unit, we will be exploring the issue of poverty and studying its impact on our state and in our community. This study will involve doing research, reading articles and news reports, and watching films and documentaries about people living in poverty. The task will culminate in writing of a research report on the topic of poverty and completion of a community service project designed to serve people living in poverty."

Next, present students with a list of goals and tasks:

- Learn to use the Gale and EBSCO databases and other resources to search for sources and do library research.
- Read various articles and reports related to poverty.
- Explore the websites of various local service organizations, such as Marion-Polk Food Share (MAPS), Union Gospel Mission, and United Way (substitute the names of your own local service organizations).
- Watch news reports, films, and movies on the issue of poverty, and take notes on them.

- Attend a class presentation by a guest speaker and take notes.
- Interview a homeless person or another individual who lives in poverty, someone who has been impacted by poverty, or someone with expert knowledge about poverty, and record or take notes on their comments.
- Learn to take notes and cite sources using correct MLA documentation style.
- Write a research report of approximately five pages on the issue of poverty and how it affects our state and community.
- Participate individually or with a group to complete at least seven hours of community service with an organization that works to combat poverty and hunger. You must complete the form for documenting your community service, and it must be signed by the supervisor.

Students were also presented with a list of research questions they could use to find a direction for their research:

1. What is poverty?
2. How is poverty defined or determined?
3. How serious a problem is poverty?
4. What do you think are the living conditions of a family living in poverty?
5. What are the causes of poverty?
6. How can poverty be prevented?
7. What does the government do about the issue of poverty?
8. What is the current minimum wage in the United States? In Oregon?
9. How much money would a person making minimum wage earn in a week? A month?
10. What can individual people and groups do about poverty in their community?
11. What are the rates of poverty in Oregon?
12. How does Oregon compare with other states in terms of numbers of people living in poverty?
13. What resources are available in Marion County for those living with poverty?
14. How are poverty and homelessness related?
15. What are the effects of poverty on children?
16. What are the effects of poverty on students?
17. What is food insecurity? How many people in our community and state are affected by it?
18. What forms of welfare and food aid are available to those living in poverty?

We also created a list of several local service organizations that students could investigate in order to complete their community service component. You could easily come up with a similar list of agencies in your own community:

- Marion-Polk Food Share
- United Way of the Mid-Willamette Valley
- Helping Hands
- The Salvation Army
- Union Gospel Mission
- Hands On, Mid-Willamette Valley
- Stand for Children
- St. Vincent de Paul Society
- Catholic Community Services
- Mano a Mano
- Family Building Blocks
- Salem-Keizer Education Foundation
- Home Youth and Resource Center
- Teen Challenge
- HOST Youth and Family Program
- Mid-Valley Community Action Agency
- Building Bridges

During the next several class periods, lessons were conducted to teach students how to use the databases, find sources, take notes, and use MLA form correctly. Students spent a few class periods working in the library and gathering information. A couple of reports related to poverty in the state of Oregon were read and discussed, and the class watched documentary films and a recent news report about poverty. (There is a great thirty-minute documentary film called "Poor America" available at http://topdocumentaryfilms.com/.) Students took notes and used these films as sources in their papers as well.

Students were to identify an agency through which they could work to complete their community service and, when necessary, were provided assistance to help them connect with these organizations. Students also had to come up with an appropriate interview source. They were expected to contact the source and conduct the interview on their own time. Several parents helped facilitate this part of the project. One of our guest speakers was a person who had been homeless at one time; another was a person who works with a local service agency. Of course, if you are also using an anchor text as part of this project, you will want to engage students in reading and discussion of the text or texts.

Students spent a few class periods writing their paper, and as a culminating activity, they prepared a presentation for the class in order to share their research, reflect on their experiences, and discuss what they had learned from this project. This project was an eye-opening experience for many students. It helped students to build and polish their literacy skills through reading, research, writing, and oral communication as well as gain greater understanding on the issue of poverty and its effects. It is indeed a time-consuming performance task, but it proved successful in teaching students academic and research skills as well as providing them with a powerful, real-world learning and service experience. In addition, it accomplished the goal of raising students' levels of consciousness about poverty and those who live with its effects.

Afterword
Letting Our Garden Grow

Whenever I walk through a beautifully-designed and well-tended garden, I am always amazed by the variety and diversity. A wide array of beautiful plants and flowers grow, both large and small, each contributing to the overall aesthetic effect. Much like the garden, our classrooms are also filled with diversity, each student unique and beautiful in his or her own way, with a variety of needs and a range of abilities and talents. Each student has the potential to grow just like each individual plant in our garden. All plants are not the same; some have different needs, much like our students. As different plants need different climates, care, and nourishment, our students also come to us with varying backgrounds, learning styles, and abilities, but all with great academic potential to learn and grow.

Like the successful gardener, the teacher must try to meet the needs of all of her or his students. This requires acknowledging that students grow at different rates; not all students learn in the same ways and within the same timelines. The steady hand of the teacher must create a classroom learning environment and rich learning tasks that can help all students grow.

English language arts teachers today typically face classrooms full of students with a broad range of literacy skills. Some will be struggling readers, some proficient readers, some highly literate. Hopefully, the strategies and materials in this book have given you some ideas and prepared you to better help your students grow and thrive, challenging them and moving them forward in their development of twenty-first-century literacy skills.

Literacy learning is the key to learning in all areas of the curriculum and life. The diverse groups of students in our classrooms today will become the next generation of leaders and citizens of tomorrow. An ancient Chinese proverb states, "A society grows great when old men plant trees whose shade they know they shall never sit in." As educators, we must sow the seeds of literacy for the next generation, to create the garden of the future that we may never see. If we strive with conviction today to plant the seeds of literacy and nourish the growth of our students, we will have succeeded in building a strong legacy for the future.

References

Arpajian-Jolley, S. (2014). How have we been standardized? Let me count the ways. *English Journal, 104*(2), 80–85.
Beers, K., & Probst, R. E. (2013). *Notice and note: Strategies for close reading.* Portsmouth, NH: Heinemann.
Berliner, D. C., & Glass, G. V. (2015). Trust but verify. *Educational Leadership, 72*(5), 10–14.
Berry, G. (2014*). Literacy for learning: A handbook of content-area strategies for middle and high school teachers.* Lanham, MD: Rowman & Littlefield.
Booth Olson, C. (2003). *The reading/writing connection: Strategies for teaching and learning in the secondary classroom.* Boston: Pearson/Allyn and Bacon.
Boyd, L. (2015). Common core in the classroom: New standards help teachers create effective lesson plans. *Education Next, 15*(1), 84.
Boyles, N. (2013). Closing in on close reading. *Educational Leadership, 70*(4), 36–41.
Bradbury, R. (1953, 1987*). Fahrenheit 451.* New York: Ballantine.
Brophy, J. (2010). *Motivating students to learn.* New York: Routledge.
Chun, M. (2010). Taking teaching to (performance) task: Linking pedagogical and assessment practices. *Change, 42*(2), 22–29.
Colding, H. D. (2016). Integrating a layered curriculum to facilitate differentiated instruction. *ASCD Express.* Retrieved from http://www.ascd.org/ascd-express/vol3/324-colding.aspx.
Cole, J. E. (2014). Motivating students to engage in close reading. *Illinois Reading Council Journal, 42*(4), 19–28.
Coleman, D., & Pimentel, S. (2012). Revised publishers' criteria for the Common Core State Standards in English Language Arts and Literacy, Grades 3–12. Retrieved from http://www.nassp.org/Content/158/pl_feb12_goldenberg.pdf.
Coleman, R., & Goldenberg, C. (2012, Feb.) The common core challenge for English language learners (ELLS). *Principal Leadership, 12*(6), 46+. Retrieved from http://go.galegroup.com/ps/i.do?.

Council of Chief State School Officers and National Governors Association. (2010). Common Core State Standards for English Language Arts and Literacy in History, Social Studies, Science and Technical Subjects. Retrieved from http://www.cdl.org/articles/common-core-state-standards-for-english-language-arts-literacy/.

Cuban, L. (1990). Reforming again, again, and again. *Educational Researcher, 19*(1), 3–13.

Davey, B. (1983). Think aloud: Modeling the cognitive process of reading comprehension. *Journal of Reading, 27*(1), 44–47.

Davis, L. (Ed.) (2013). *Common Core literacy lesson plans: Ready-to-use resources, 9–12*. Larchmont, NY: Eye on Education.

Del Guidice, M., & Luna, R. (2013). Cut to the core. *Publishers Weekly, 260*(36), 22.

Dewey, J. (1972). *John Dewey, the early works 1882–1898: Early Essays* (Vol. 5). Carbondale, IL: Southern Illinois University Press.

Eppley, K. (2015). Seven traps of the Common Core State Standards. *Journal of adolescent and adult literacy, 59*(2), 207–16. doi:10.1002/jaal.431.

Frey, N., & Fisher, D. (2013). *Rigorous reading: 5 access points for comprehending complex texts*. Thousand Oaks, CA: Corwin.

Gallagher, K. (2003). *Reading reasons: Motivational mini-lessons for middle and high school*. Portland, ME: Stenhouse.

Gallagher, K. (2015). *In the best interest of students: Staying true to what works in the ELA classroom*. Portland, ME: Stenhouse.

Gorlewski, J., & Gorlewski, D. (2014). From the editors. *English Journal, 104*(2), 11–12.

Herbert, M. (2011, Feb.). Common Core's implications for special ed students. *District Administration, 47*(2), 10.

Heyck, D. L. D. (1994). *Barrios and borderlands: Cultures of Latinos and Latinas in the United States*. New York: Routledge.

Hilsenrath, J. (2015, July 30). Fed preps careful path for rate hike. *The Wall Street Journal*, A1.

Jago, C. (2011). *With rigor for all: Meeting Common Core Standards for Reading Literature* (2nd ed.). Portsmouth, NH: Heinemann.

Jay, J. (1787). *Federalist* No. 2: Concerning dangers from foreign force and influence. Retrieved from http://thefederalistpapers.org/federalist-papers/the-federalist-no-2-concerning-dangers-from-foreign-force-and-influence.

Kennedy, X. J., & Gioia, D. (2010). *An introduction to fiction* (11th ed.). Boston: Longman.

LeMaster, J. (2009). *Critical reading: Deep reading strategies for expository texts, teacher's guide 7–12*. San Diego, CA: AVID Press.

McCarter, J. (2009, Jan. 28). Something Wilder. *Newsweek, 154*(13), 64.

McTigue, J. (2015). What is a performance task? Defined learning blog. Retrieved from https://blog.performancetask.com/what-is-a-performance-task-part-1-9faO-d99ead3b.

Orwell, G. (1949, 1977). *1984*. New York: Signet/Penguin Classics.

Partnership for Assessment of Readiness for College and Careers. (2011). PARCC model content frameworks: English language arts/literacy grades 3–11. Retrieved from http://parcc-assessment.org/resources/educator-resources/model-content-frameworks.

Rosenblatt, L. (1976). *The reader, the text, the poem: The transactional theory of the literary work.* Carbondale, IL: Southern Illinois University Press.

Rosevear, J. (2015). Better together: Pairing fiction and nonfiction in the high school classroom. Blog: We Are Teachers. Retrieved from http://www.weareteachers.com/better-together-pairing-fiction-and-nonfiction-in-the-high-school-classroom.

Rycik, J. A. (2014). News and views: Support continues to erode for Common Core Standards and assessment. *American Secondary Education, 42*(3), 52–54.

Simpson, A., Walsh, M., & Rowsell, J. (2013). The digital reading path: Researching modes and multidirectionality with iPads. *Literacy 47*(3), 123–30.

Stotsky, S. (2013). What's wrong with Common Core ELA Standards? Center for Education Reform. Retrieved from http://www.edreform.com/2013/02/whats-wrong-with-common-core-ela-standards/.

Strauss, V. (2014). Answer sheet: Four Common Core "flimflams." *The Washington Post.* Retrieved from http://www.washingtonpost.com/blogs.

Sullivan, N. (Ed.) (1978). *The treasury of American poetry.* Garden City, NY: International Collectors Library.

The Every Student Succeeds Act: Explained. (2015, Dec. 7). *Education Week.* Retrieved from http://www.edweek.org/ew/articles/2015/12/07/the-every-student-succeeds-act-explained.html.

The write path in English language arts: Exploring texts with strategic reading. (2012). San Diego: AVID Press.

Tienken, C. H. (2012). The Common Core State Standards: The emperor is still looking for his clothes. *Kappa Delta Pi Record, 48*(4), 152–55. doi:10.1080/00228958.2012.733928.

Tienken, C. H. (2014). Non-standardized standards. *Kappa Delta Pi Record, 50*(2), 56–60. doi:10.1080/00228958.2014.900844.

Tierney, R. J., & Shanahan, T. (1991). Research on the reading-writing relationship: Interactions, transactions, and outcomes. In R. Barr, M. Kamil, P. Mosenthal, & P. D. Pearson (Eds.). *Handbook of reading research* (Vol. 2, pp. 246–80). New York: Longman.

Vick, K. (2015, April 6). Cuba on the cusp: As U.S. policy softens, the island that time forgot prepares for change. *Time, 185*(12), 28–39.

Walker, A. (2008). In search of our mothers' gardens. In *The Seagull Reader: Essays* (2nd ed., pp. 350–61). New York: W.W. Norton.

Wingert, P. (2014, Jan. 2). The Common Core is tough on kids who are still learning English. *The Atlantic.* Retrieved from http://www.theatlantic.com/education/archive/2014/01/the-common-core-is-tough-on-kids-who-are-still-learning-english/282712/.

Index

1984 (Orwell): and the think aloud, 27–28

accountability, in education, 10
academic vocabulary, 9, 13, 19. *See also* domain specific vocabulary
Accelerated Speed Reading Trainer (app), 64–65
active reading, 24–25, 42, 44–45, 88. *See also* text marking
analyzing a source strategy, 59–61; procedure for teaching, 60–61
anchor texts, 19, 92
apps, for reading, 64–66
assessments, and curriculum, 5, 9
Audiobooks—Classics for Free (app), 65–66
authorial craft, 21, 39, 42, 46–51, 56–58
AVID program, 39, 59–60, 66, 139

The Bean Trees (Kingsolver): characters and themes, 125–26; essay prompts, 127–28; lesson sequence, 127–29; performance task, 125–29; related standards, 126; supplementary readings, 126–29
Bloom's Taxonomy, 51
Books—23,469 Classics to Go (app), 66

Bradbury, Ray. *See Fahrenheit 451* (Bradbury)

Catcher in the Rye (Salinger), 74, 76–77, 122
Carol, Lewis. *See* "Jabberwocky"
charting the text strategy, 34–4; charting the text table, *41*; procedure for teaching, 39–42
Cisneros, Sandra. *See House on Mango Street* (Cisneros)
"Civil Disobedience" (Thoreau), 63
claims and counterclaims, 73, 78
close reading, xiv, 8, 19–21, 24–25, 36, 59, 61, 67, 79; across disciplines, 21; controversy over, 21–23; definition of, 19–20; and vocabulary, 28–29
Cody, Robin. *See Ricochet River* (Cody)
coherence, in writing, 82
collaboration, 9, 21, 48, 52, 60, 78
College Reading Comprehension (app), 66
color-coding of text, 54–55; color-coding activity sheet, *79*; example of, 55–56; procedure for teaching, 55–56; teaching strategy, 78–79
commentary strategy, 56–59; central assertion, 58; evaluation/scoring of, 58–59; mini-commentary, 59;

oral and written, 56; procedure for teaching, 57–59
Common Core State Standards, xiii, 3–4, 10–12, 18–20, 37, 48, 50, 56, 93; 70/30 ratio, 11–12; anchor standards, 4–19; close reading, 21–23, 37; controversy over, 4–8; complex text, 23–24; creativity, 6; criticism by experts, 6–7; cross-disciplinary approach, 18–19; curriculum alignment, 10; developmental appropriateness, 6–7; equity, 6; history of, 4–5; implementation of, 4; increasing level of complexity, 8; informational text, 10–13; in states, 4, 7; language standards, 9; literature standards, 10–16; media and technology standards, 9–10; misinterpretations of, 11–12; politics of, 4–8; rigor, 7–8; shifts in, 8–10; speaking and listening standards, 9, 74–75; testing of, 4–5; textbooks, 7; textual evidence, 73–75, 88–89; writing standards, 9, 74–75
complex text, 8, 13, 19, 20, 23–25, 45–46, 52; definition of, 23–25; qualitative and quantitative indicators, 24
comprehension, monitoring of, 25
context clues, 29–30; examples of, 30; teaching, 30–31
craft and structure, in writing, 31–32, 51
critical reading, and AVID, 39
The Crucible (Miller): background, 119; essay topics, 121; lesson sequence, 121–22; performance task, 119–22; Puritan language, 119–20; related standards, 120; supplementary readings, 120
Cuban, Larry, 2–4
Cummings, e. e. *See* "i thank You God for most this amazing"
curriculum, ELA, 10–16
Cyrano de Bergerac (Rostand): essay outline, 104; lesson sequence, 102–5; performance task, 98, 102–5; related standards, 102; summary, 98; supplementary readings, 103

definition essay, 98–102
discussion, academic, 9
domain-specific vocabulary, 9, 19

elaboration of evidence, 76, 78, 82
Elementary and Secondary Reauthorization Act, 7
English language arts (ELA), 10–11
evaluation systems, 3
Every Student Succeeds Act (ESSA), 7
evidence, *See* textual evidence

Fahrenheit 451 (Bradbury), 43–44, 92–93
The Federalist, No. 2 (Jay), 52
Fitzgerald, F. Scott. *See The Great Gatsby* (Fitzgerald)
Fortey, Cara, 98, 123
four basic questions strategy, 25; figure for, *26*
four corners of the text, 20, 21–23, 50

Gale databases, 60
Gallagher, Kelly, 8, 10, 14, 24; and CCSS reading standards, 8; *In the Best Interest of Students*, 10, 12–13, 31
gardening metaphor, ix
globalization, 2
Google Classroom, 65
Graham, Sandy, 113, 119
The Great Gatsby (Fitzgerald): background, 105–6; essay topics, 107–8; lesson sequence, 107–9; one-pager activity, 67, *70–71*; performance task, 105–9; related standards, 106–7; supplementary readings, 106–7

high-frequency verbs, 40
high-stakes tests, 25
House on Mango Street (Cisneros): background and characters,

129–30; essay prompt, 132; lesson sequence, 131–33; performance task, 129–33; related standards, 130; supplementary readings, 130–31

Huckleberry Finn, The Adventures of (Twain): importance of, 94; language and dialect, 94; lesson sequence, 95–98; performance task, 77, 93–98; student papers, *99–102*; supplementary readings, 95; themes, 94

"i thank You God for most this amazing" (Cummings), 32–33
"In Search of Our Mother's Gardens" (Walker), 36
inferences, drawing of, 48–49
infographics, 93
informational text, 11–12, 13, 19 59; examples of, 54, 59
inquiry, and reading, 20–21
integrating ideas, 51
integrating language arts skills, ix, 17–19; and Common Core, 18–19
interactive shared reading strategy, 42–44; benefits of, 42; example of, 43–44
International Baccalaureate (IB) Program, 56–57, 79
Isom, Matthew, 79, 81, 126

"Jabberwocky" (Carol), 16
Jago, Carol, 13
Jay, John. *See The Federalist*, No. 2 (Jay)
journal writing/entries, 60

Kingslover, Barbara. *See The Bean Trees* (Kingslover)
KNOWS strategy, 63–64; example of, 63–64; procedure for teaching, 63

language arts skills, 17–18. S*ee also* English Language Arts (ELA)
layered curriculum for poetry, 136–39; A, B, C layers, 137; assignment sheet, *138–39*; definition of, 136–37; and learning styles, 136–37; procedure for teaching, 137–39; teacher as facilitator, 137
literacy, and academic disciplines, 7–8
literacy learning, xiii, 10
literacy skills, importance of, x, 2
literary analysis of theme in poetry, 133–36; essay prompt, 134; lesson sequence, 134–36; outline format, 135; poems about death, 134; related standards, 133; rubric for revising, 136
literary terms, 57
literary text, 24
literature, xiii-iv; classic texts, 13; Common Core, 10–16; critical thinking, 16; diversity, 15; human experience, 16; imagination/creativity, 15; important role of, 12–16; pleasure/escape, 16; rationale for, 14–16; research on, 13, 15; sensitivity to language, 15; vocabulary/speaking skills, 15
Longfellow, H. W. *See* "Mezzo Cammin" (Longfellow)

Macbeth (Shakespeare), 92–93
making connections, in reading, 45
margin notes. *See* text marking
"Mezzo Cammin" (Longfellow), 55
Miller, Arthur. *See The Crucible* (Miller)
monitoring comprehension strategy, 44–45; examples, 45; chart, *46*
motivation, and close reading, 20–21, 24
multiple intelligences, 136
multiple readings, 24, 42, 45, 52, 57, 77; strategy for teaching, 45–47

NEWSELA, online and app versions, 65
Newsweek magazine, 88

"O Captain! My Captain" (Whitman), *81*
Obama, Barack, 7
Of Mice and Men (Steinbeck): background and characters, 113;

essay topics, 114–15; introductory paragraph, *118*; lesson sequence, 114–19; performance task, 113–19; planning sheet, *116*; related standards, 113; supplementary readings, 113–14
one-pager strategy, 66–71, 132; assignment sheets, *68–69*; for informational text, 69; for literary text, 68; procedure for teaching, 66–67; student examples, *70–71*
opt-out movements, and Common Core, 5
organization and structure of text, 53–54. See also text structure strategy
organization, in writing, 81–83
Orwell, George. See *1984* (Orwell)
Our Town (Wilder): background and themes, 109; essay topics, 111–12; lesson sequence, 110–13; performance task, 109–13; related standards, 109–10; supplementary readings, 110
outlines, 77
OUTREAD Speedreading app, 65

paraphrasing strategy, 61–63; procedure for teaching, 62; in research writing, 61
PARCC (Partnership for Assessment of Readiness for College and Careers), 4–5, 20
PARCC test, 76
performance tasks, xiii, xiv, 13, 19, 89, 91–93; definition of, 91–93; for specific anchor texts, 93–133; procedure for designing, 93. See also *The Bean Trees* (Kingsolver); *The Crucible* (Miller); *Cyrano de Bergerac* (Rostand); *The Great Gatsby* (Fitzgerald); *House on Mango Street* (Cisneros); *Huckleberry Finn, The Adventures of* (Twain); *Of Mice and Men* (Steinbeck); *Our Town* (Wilder); poverty performance task; *Ricochet River* (Cody)
poetry explication activity, 79–81; visual for, *80–81*
poverty performance task, 133–39; community service, 143; culminating activity, 144; films, 143; goals and tasks, 141–42; guest speakers, 140; literary selections for, 140–41; overview of assignment, 141; related standards, 140; research questions, 142; research skills, 139, 143; service organizations, 143
prefixes, suffixes, and roots, 29
Prep4SAT Reading app, 65
previewing, 45
prior knowledge, 63
professional learning communities (PLC), 78
punctuation marks, 34–35
punctuation and reading, 32–37; manipulation of, 32–33

"A Quilt for the Country" (Quindlen), 88
Quindlen, Anna. See "A Quilt for the Country" (Quindlen)

readability, in text, 24
reading, and Common Core, 8, 12–13; importance of, 14–16; increasing level of complexity, 8
reading comprehension, 66
"reading like a writer" strategy, 31–37
reading process, 22–23; and background information/prior knowledge, 22–23; and text marking, 37–38
reading, purpose for, 77
reading stamina, 24
reform, educational, 1–4; cycles of change, 2–4; movements, 1, 7; and schools, 2–3
repeated readings. See multiple readings.

re-reading. *See* multiple readings
research writing, 9
Revised Publisher's Criteria for the Common Core, 11–12; and close reading, 11, 22–23; and literary nonfiction, 12; and literature, 11–12; and textual evidence, 75
Ricochet River (Cody): background and history, 122–23; Celilo Falls, 122–23; essay prompts, 124–25; lesson sequence, 124–25; performance task, 122–25; related standards, 123; supplementary readings, 123–24
Rosenblatt, Louise, 22, 23
Rostand, Edmond. *See Cyrano de Bergerac* (Rostand)

Salinger, J. D. *See Cather in the Rye* (Salinger)
SAT Prep by Ready4SAT app, 65
SBA (Smarter Balanced Assessment) test, 76
SBA argument writing rubric, 76, 78
SBAC (Smarter Balanced Assessment Consortium), 45
scaffolding, 18, 46
sentence structure, and reading, 32
Shakespeare, William. *See Macbeth* (Shakespeare)
source material, 59–61
special education students, 6
standardization, 4
standardized testing, 3
standards, xiii, 4–8, 91; and policymakers, 56; and teachers, 5
Steinbeck, John. *See Of Mice and Men* (Steinbeck)
storytelling, 14
structural analysis, 29
struggling readers, 22–23
student-determined text-dependent questions, 50–52
summarizing, 45
synthesizing sources, 20, 24, 92

teaching text structure. *See* text structure
technology, 2; and literacy, 64
text complexity. *See* complex text
text-dependent questions, 50–52, 75, 88
text marking, 37–39, 57, 60, 77; and annotation, 37; patterns of, 53; procedure for teaching, 37–38
text structure strategy, 52–54
textual evidence, 48–49, 73–76; defined, 75–76; teaching of, 76–78
theme, in literature, 131
think-aloud strategy, 25–28; example of, 27–28; procedure for teaching, 26–27
Thoreau, Henry David. *See* "Civil Disobedience" (Thoreau)
"A Time to Dig Deeper" strategy, 87–89; handout for, *89*; procedure for teaching, 88
transitions, 81–87; list of common, 82, 97; transitions activity, *83–87*
turnitin.com, 93
Twain, Mark. *See Huckleberry Finn, The Adventures of* (Twain)
two-column notes, 48–49

using evidence from text strategy, 48–50; graphic organizer, *49*; procedure for teaching, 48–49

vocabulary: critical vocabulary, 45; structural analysis and context clues, 28–31
vocabulary instruction, 9, 46

Walker, Alice. *See* "In Search of Our Mother's Gardens" (Walker)
Whitman, Walt. *See* "O Captain! My Captain" (Whitman)
Wilder, Thornton. *See Our Town* (Wilder)
Word parts, 29
writing across the curriculum, 9
writing, argument, 9
writing rubrics, 93, 98, 113, 115, 122, 129

About the Author

Gregory Berry teaches English at South Salem High School, where he has also served as teacher leader, instructional coach, and department coordinator, and is an adjunct English instructor at Chemeketa Community College. He received his BA in English, BS in Education, and MS is education from Eastern Oregon University and his doctorate in educational leadership, curriculum, and instruction from Portland State University in 2009. He is the author of *Literacy for Learning: A Handbook of Content Area Strategies for Middle and High School Teachers,* published by Rowman & Littlefield in 2014.